Drink Fine Wine...
Ride Fine Horses

Leading the Life of Your Dreams

Tammy
RIMES

Drink Fine Wine... Ride Fine Horses
Leading the Life of Your Dreams
Copyright ©2013 Tammy Rimes

Published by Crystal Pointe Media Inc.
San Diego, California

ISBN-13: 978-1-492880-14-1

Editor: Tyler Tichelaar
Cover & Interior Design: Fusion Creative Works, fusioncw.com
Cover Photography: April Visel Photography
Featured horse is RCh Ventarrones owned by Rancho Chahuchu

For additional copies please visit: www.sdwinery.com

Testimonials

Praise for *Drink Fine Wine...Ride Fine Horses:*

"Tammy Rimes masters the message that anyone who has lost or forgotten his or her dreams needs to hear. If you have steered away from your dreams, Rimes has captured the essence of how to get right back on the road to remember that they absolutely do matter, and to start to live your life again."

— Sharita Star, Life Coach, Speaker & Author

"Dreaming about a dream life is easy, but making it happen takes a plan, and then doing what is necessary to execute that plan. Tammy Rimes shares her own life story, as well as the achievements of others, to demonstrate practical ways to move toward your own dream life."

—Patrick Snow, International Best-Selling Author of *Creating Your Own Destiny* and *The Affluent Entrepreneur*

"Tammy shares true stories as examples of the power of living your dreams in a way that inspires you to dream big, believe in yourself, and follow your passion. Her words and her message are clear and powerful. If you are ready to start living the life of your dreams, this book is for you!"

—Mark Porteous, Author of *Maximizing Your Human Experience: Seven Powerful Tools to Navigate through Your Journey of Life*

"Tammy is someone to watch and listen to as she is practicing what she teaches, and has lived her dream. If I were to assign one adjective to her work, it would be 'Inspirational.'"

—**Lisa Bentson, CEO Leads Club Inc. and Author of** *Focused Networking: The Eight Principles of 20th Century Marketing*

"A powerful book that's 100% inspiration and motivation to take charge and do what you've always dreamed you would do!"

—**Michelle Bergquist, author of** *How to Build a Million Dollar Database*

"Tammy Rimes's *Drink Fine Wine...Ride Fine Horses* is a must read for people who want to live life to the fullest and accomplish their dreams to the best of their potential."

—**Seconde Nimenya, author of** *Evolving Through Adversity*

"In her book *Drink Fine Wine...Ride Fine Horses*, Tammy Rimes' inspirational stories will show you how to lead the life of your dreams."

—**H. C. Joe Raymond, Speaker, Personal Coach, and Author** **of** *Embracing Change from the Inside Out*

Dedication

To my mother, Lessie Rimes,
who always has ultimate faith in me.

She calls me her hero; however,
she is really the hero in my life.

Acknowledgments

It takes a village to create a Dream Life, and it took a village to write this book. Special thanks to my husband William Holzhauer, who has supported and encouraged me with anything that I've ever wanted to do, including the dream to write this book. Our children, Saum, Shireen, and Jonathan have been a great part of this journey and have all worked toward creating this special family. They have been there since the beginning—through the home remodeling, moves, long hours, and missed school events, and they have worked at helping with stages of creating our Dream Life. William and I are so proud of the young adults whom our children have become.

Our winery, horse ranch, and life could not be successful without the help and love of all our friends, extended family, and customers. In preparation for the Grand Opening event for our second tasting room in Ramona, we pushed hard to complete the construction and landscaping on time. With hundreds of people coming, there was much to do during the weeks leading up the event. William and I were putting in long 12-14 hour days. The day prior to the ribbon cutting ceremony, I had to rush William to the emergency room for medical complications. As we were sitting there, I was contemplating how to move a hospital bed into the winery building during the grand opening ceremony, so William could enjoy the festivities. We had worked so hard and for so long that I did not want him to miss it. I figured he could sit on a bed in the winery and have everyone come up to visit with him...sort of like they do for visiting heads of state! At this point, there was no cancelling the party, with people coming in from all over the country.

As my family and friends arrived at the ranch that same day, they instantly went to work—labeling bottles of wine, setting up the gift shop, hanging the gate, marking the parking lot, and completing the decorations. We could not have done it without them. Over 450 people attended the Grand Opening event, and William was able to be part of it. My heartfelt thanks to my brothers John and Jeff, my mother and father Lessie and John Rimes, my sister-in-law Betty, and my true friends Jennifer and Ed Casamassima and Sean and Donna Shirashi—we could not have done all of this without your love, support, and quite a bit of elbow grease.

When you are on top of the world and living the dream, it's easy to have lots of friends. But it's when you are working toward the dream—and especially when you call someone from an emergency room for help—that you truly know who your friends and family are.

Contents

Preface

Fifteen years ago, my husband and I were raising three pre-teens in a fixer home, with a vision of having something bigger. We both wanted a place with some land, and I wanted horses, having been horse crazy as a young girl. Two marriages, kids, and responsibilities had taken me away from horses and into the world of making a living, working a steady government job, paying the bills, and keeping up with everyone's activities.

We looked intermittently for years, but we could not quite find the right property; nor did we have enough money for the down payment. However, we already had the name chosen for our future ranch "Hacienda de las Rosas" or "Big House of the Roses." When people asked me where it was located, I would point to my head and say, "Right here...but one day it will be a real place." Many years went by while we remodeled our "fixer" house and raised our children. The ranch and house of our dreams were always in the background.

One long weekend, my parents were visiting from Florida. I decided to take them on a long drive to Ramona, a lovely rural area north of San Diego, to show them where we might have our dream ranch of the future. After three hours in the car together, I decided it was time to head back home. As I was starting to drive out of Ramona, my father pointed toward a "For Sale" sign and said, "Let's go drive by that one." I was tired but agreed, "Okay, but this is the last one." The sign had a pamphlet box, which was empty, and there was no description of the house. We decided to drive up the long driveway since the house could not be seen from the road. As I rounded the corner, there was a man standing in the middle of the driveway. I screeched to a stop, quickly opening my window to apologize and say that we were just driving by and didn't mean to disturb him.

That did not stop my dad, who had already opened his door and was walking toward the man with an outstretched hand. Being from the South, my dad assumed that drop-bys were always welcome, even if we were total strangers. The man shook my dad's hand, and within moments, they both shared that they were retired pilots, and the man was inviting my mom and me out of the car to see the house. Walking up to the Spanish adobe home, with a beautiful courtyard and rose garden in front, I finally saw our vision of "Hacienda de las Rosas" there before us. Through a huge rounded oak door entrance, we walked into the house, and without knowing how many bedrooms there were or any other details about the house and property, I knew this was the place. We took a quick tour and then excused ourselves, thanking him for his time.

As we were getting into the car, the seller mentioned that this house had been on the market for almost a year, but it would be listed on the front page of the next day's Sunday paper as the featured home in the San Diego real estate section. When I got home,

I told my husband that I had found *the* house, and he called to make an appointment the next morning. The seller said that he went to church early, but my husband, who was a realtor, could come by and check out the house. My husband and I arrived very early before the seller left, took a five-minute walk through the house, and went outside to complete the paperwork. My husband had a saying with his clients, "If you walk in a place and you hear the angels sing, then it's your home." Well, we both heard a loud Hallelujah chorus singing in our heads and knew this house was THE ONE. The real estate office opened at 9 a.m., and as its front door was being unlocked, we arrived with a signed offer for full price. My father scoffed at us for offering full price and asked why we didn't negotiate for a lower price. However, we knew this was the home we had talked about, worked for, and dreamed about for the last ten years, so we did not want to take a chance on losing it.

The seller accepted our offer, but he wanted a very large down payment, which we did not have. So we pulled all the equity out of our current home (not even listed for sale yet!) and put the money down. We quickly listed our current home, and spent a very scary four months paying three mortgages—one on the new house, and two on the old house. When we finally sold the old house, we breathed a huge sigh of relief. We now owned our dream home…a lovely Spanish adobe house with an aging avocado grove and 600 dead apple trees.

If you think that's the end of the dream…it's only the beginning. Since that time, we have developed a successful horse ranch, a winery with two tasting room locations, and a very full life. People often tell us, "You are living the life." Some days, I look at them and think, "If you only realized how hard this is and how tired I am." But deep down, I know we are living the life, and we wouldn't have it any other way. People share with me, "It's always been my dream to _____," with them filling in the blank. I reply, "Well, then just do it." Many look at me in disbelief, or they give me some reason or excuse why it can't happen for them.

We all have a vision of our Dream Life. We have an image of the life we want to live, the friends and family relationships we want to have, and the home and environment where we want to be. And if my husband and I can do it, then anyone can. Let me take you on a journey through the next several chapters to share how we did it, in hopes that those lessons will help you on your own trek toward your Dream Life.

Chapter 1

Dreaming the Dream Life

"Keep your dreams alive. Understand to achieve anything requires faith and belief in yourself, vision, hard work, determination, and dedication. Remember all things are possible for those who believe."
Gail Devers, Three Time U.S. Olympic Champion

If you had all the money, time, and resources in the world, what would you do with your life? Would you be living in the house and community where you are living now? Would you be surrounded by the people whom you currently work and interact with? Would you be wearing the same clothes, driving the same car, spending your day the same way? Would you be the same person? The answer is probably "No" for most people. And why is that? Why aren't more of us living our dreams?

Well, it takes courage to live your dream. And it takes creativity...and hard work...and sometimes, money and resources. It takes rearranging your focus, your priorities, your time, and where your energy is spent. How many people do that? How many people honestly dream and live their passions? Before the ancient Hebrews saw the Promised Land, they believed in it. Most of the world's top athletes dreamed about scoring touchdowns and goals while playing as children. Successful entrepreneurs who started their businesses from scratch started with dreams. If you want something... you need to dream first. You need to believe it before you see it.

One evening, when I was flying home from a business trip, a young man sitting next to me was wearing shorts and sandals with Band-Aids on most of his toes. After the plane took off, I pointed to his feet and asked him whether he had been in a skateboard accident. He laughed and said, "No, I just finished climbing Mt. Rainier, and now I'm going home to celebrate with my dad." I was fascinated and asked him about the trip and what it took to prepare. He was enthusiastic and eager to share his story. He replied that a couple of years earlier, he had read a book by a famous mountaineer, who had climbed most of the world's tallest peaks. After reading the book, he knew this was his dream—to climb mountains! So, he took rock climbing lessons, interned with a couple of seasoned guides, and started on a training program to prepare. Although he lived in San Diego, which is certainly not known for any mountains, he would hike long distances to condition himself. He would walk the long beach shoreline in his hiking boots and a backpack filled with 90 lbs. of rocks. Sometimes these hikes would be 5-6 hours long. His goal for later that year was to climb Mt. McKinley in Alaska. This Mt. Rainier climb had been a training run for him. His ultimate goal was to conquer and climb the highest mountain peaks around the world. He explained the process of going up the mountain and the precautions that were taken. Coming down the mountain is done at a much more relaxed pace. Those on their way down often greet climbers on their way up the mountain to share any knowledge or insight about that day's conditions. He said that at one particular point, he saw two men approaching and immediately recognized one of them as the author of the book that first piqued his interest in mountain climbing. He immediately put out his hand, and told the world famous climber that he was the young man's inspiration. Then he pulled the book out of his backpack...he always carried it when climbing to read on the long nights when camping in the mountains. The author signed his book, adding an amazing personal message that included the words "Keep climbing." What a cool experience... actually to meet the person who originally inspired your dream. I asked the young man if he had a real job too, and he replied, "Oh yes, but it is to pay the bills and finance my dream."

You may be thinking, "I don't know what my Dream Life is." But I would argue that you do. However, over time and distance, it has been pushed down, forgotten, ignored, until you think it is just a childish fairy tale and not a dream. Most adults have gotten out of the habit of dreaming. And many don't think they can dream anymore.

My childhood dream was to own a horse ranch. Not as a hobby, but as a business and as a lifestyle. I would make up names for my horses, write out stable and feeding plans, read horse journals, study the different breeds, and determine ways to generate an income. And this was while I was in elementary school! I had an old quarter horse as a child, but he stayed at my grandparents' place, which was six hours away. During summer vacations, I would spend all my time with this horse, tracking his feeding, riding, and grooming schedules. My best summer memories were long trail rides in the woods of northern Florida. I would fantasize about my future ranch, the foals I would raise, and the people who would come to enjoy this life with me. When summer ended, I would return to our home in Miami; there, attending school and living in the suburbs, I couldn't wait until the Christmas holidays when I could see my horse again. While I was in high school, my dad sold my horse since it was getting old and I wasn't spending as much time going to my grandparents to visit due to school and sports activities. I decided to put my dream aside. Then college, and work, and marriage came...and the thoughts of owning a horse ranch and business went away. But it didn't really go away. It was always there... just pushed down into the background.

In his book *Put Your Dreams to the Test: 10 Questions to Help You See It and Seize It*, John C. Maxwell talks about identifying your dreams to create the life you have always wanted. Included is a long list of different kinds of dreams...material dreams, career dreams, and romantic dreams. The reader is asked to complete the list to help develop his or her life dream. Maxwell defines a dream as "an inspiring picture of the future that energizes mind, will, and emotions, empowering you to do everything you can to achieve it." The message he is sharing is that dreams don't need to be huge; however, they do need to be bigger than you are. Dreams propel and drive you forward.

Look at any group of young children at play. They can easily pretend and will tell you quickly what their future dreams are. They are going to Mars, they are going to be ballerinas, they are going to be Olympic boxing champions, they will own castles, they will be cowboys with big ranches and tigers...there is no limit to their dreams. They don't put limits on themselves. In fact, the limits will come from others—parents, teachers, friends—who tell them their dreams are dumb or unachievable. Over time, they start to scale down on the dreams or replace them with what others dream for them. Someone who wants to be an artist gets a "real" job because it's more sensible. How many young adults do you know who are pursuing a career because that's what their parents want for them?

But how do you learn to dream again? You start dreaming. I know, it sounds simple, but it's true. Dreaming makes an ordinary person live an extraordinary life. All great dreamers started living ordinary lives. Some of these ordinary people who dreamed big started with huge disadvantages. Martin Luther King Jr. had social disadvantages; Franklin D. Roosevelt had physical disadvantages; and Mother Teresa had economic disadvantages. But none of them let these disadvantages stop them from attaining their dreams. Their dreams propelled them forward.

Lucille Ball had a tough childhood. Her father died when she was three. She later lived with a stepfamily who didn't have much money, and she often commented about her poor upbringing. However, Ball wanted to be in movies, and eventually, she convinced her mother to allow her to enroll in a New York City drama school. But despite her longing to make it on the stage, Ball was a shy, tongue-tied teenager who was too nervous to draw much notice. Her teacher finally wrote to her mother that Ball was wasting her time and money. However, that did not stop Ball. She would eventually appear in seventy-two movies during her long career, including a string of second-tier films in the 1940s. Unfortunately, Ball was unable to break into the kinds of starring roles she'd always dreamed about due to Hollywood's selection process.

After Ball met and married Desi Arnaz, they started to flesh out their own plan. Arnaz pushed his wife to try broadcasting, and Ball soon landed a lead part in the radio comedy *My Favorite Husband*. The program caught the attention of CBS executives who wanted her to recreate something similar on the small screen. Ball insisted it include her real-life husband, something the network refused to do. So, Lucille walked away, and with Desi, she put together an *I Love Lucy*-like vaudeville act and took it on the road. Success soon greeted the pair. So did a contract from CBS. Ball and Arnaz knew exactly what they wanted. Their demands included the opportunity to create their new program in Hollywood rather than New York, where most television programs were still being shot. But the biggest hurdle centered on the couple's preference to film the program rather than broadcast it live. When CBS argued about the cost, Ball and Arnaz agreed to a reduction in pay while retaining full ownership rights to the program and running it under their newly formed production company, Desilu Productions. From its debut in 1951, and for the next six years, *I Love Lucy* was the number one watched show across America. Here was a woman whose talents Hollywood had been unwilling to showcase, but Ball believed in herself and her vision, becoming a television icon and one of the wealthiest and best-known women in Hollywood.

You only have this one life to live. And there are many chapters in this life. Shouldn't the ultimate ending be one where you live the life of your dreams? If others have a Dream Life, shouldn't you too?

Chapter 2

Defining Your Passion

"Whatever you think...make sure it is what you think.
Whatever you want, be sure it is what you want.
Whatever you feel, be sure it is what you feel."
T.S Eliot

Think back to what you loved to do as a child. Before some-one told you that you couldn't do that or life took over on a new path. What activities as a child are some of your fondest memories? What do you love to do now as an adult? If you had more time or money, what would you do today that you aren't already doing? If you had no other obligations, where would you like to place your focus and energy? If you only had six months left to live...what would you continue doing...what would you stop doing? If the sky were the limit, what would your passion be?

Many years ago, I worked on a small team within a large Water Utilities department. My boss planned a team retreat to focus our vision and goals for a new recycled water program. The facilitator thought the first session should be about who we are as individuals, so the team could learn more about one another. He asked everyone to pair up. Because the group had an odd number of people, I was the only one left without a partner. The facilitator offered to be my assigned partner for the exercise. He had a series of questions: "Who are you? What do you do? Tell me about your personal and professional life." I easily answered these. He then stopped me and asked a question I can still hear in my head: "Okay, you've told me your name, your job title, and how many kids you have, etc., but what about you? Who are you and what is your passion?" I just looked at him blankly, not quite understanding the question. He followed up by saying, "For me, it's creating music. I have my guitar always with me, and I love to spend hours creating and playing music, and my goal is to produce my own album. So what is your passion?" I looked at him again with the thought in my head, "Is this guy serious?" I was a newly divorced single mom with two children, one of whom was having issues at school; I was renting a small two-bedroom apartment, working a full-time job that often required overtime, and barely paying my bills each month. Who had time for a passion? I just mumbled, "Well, I like to read," and then went on to the next question.

But that evening, the question still haunted me. What was my passion? And more importantly, why didn't I seem to have one? I started to cry because I had no passion! What had happened to the girl who was in the top 10 percent of her high school class, who was president of one of the top service clubs, and first string player on both the girls soccer and basketball teams? Where was the girl who wrote plays and essays, had won a full academic scholarship to college, had been one of the few women in the early college computer classes, graduating with a computer science degree? She had big dreams and goals back then. She had lots of passion—for life, for achieving excellence, and for getting ahead…WAY ahead in life. I had dreamed of being a veterinarian and owning a horse ranch! What happened?

Well, a funny thing happens when you start living a life. Sometimes the life takes over and you become part of a path that you don't even recognize anymore. And the further you get down the path, the more you start to forget where it started, and where you were intending to go. Often, I ask people during speaking engagements to shout out what they wanted to be when they grew up when they were seven or eight years old. I often hear "fireman," "pilot," "doctor," etc. Then I ask "So why are you doing what you are doing now?" And we all have great answers: I got married, our family moved, we had kids, my mother got ill, this job just came up, etc. I'm not saying that you have to be what you dreamed about when you were young. Just look at your life and where you are now. Is this where you want to be? Is this the dream house, family, job, life that you always wanted? Do you have passion about what you do? Do you jump up in the morning, excited to start the day and get out there to live your life? If you are like most people, probably not. That's why we are talking about identifying your passion as you evaluate your life and develop your Dream Life.

During a recent vacation trip to the Lake Tahoe area, my husband went on a fishing trip with a local guide. He was in his late forties and had lived in the area most of his life. My husband asked how he became a fishing guide. He replied that he loved the life— fishing was his passion. For about 6-7 months a year, that's what he did for a living—taking tourists and visitors out to fish on the lake while also fishing himself. And he got paid for it! Imagine, going out fishing on one of the most beautiful lakes in the world as your job! He and his wife had a home in the north Lake Tahoe area. During the winter, he spent time working at one of the local ski lodges when the snow hit the area. Was he rich? Maybe not in money, but he was extremely happy and satisfied with his life. He loved living in the Lake Tahoe area, and he looked forward to waking up and going to work every day. Now, that's a life of passion.

Trusting Your Gifts

We all have special gifts. Every person is created with a specific set of chromosomes, born into a particular environment, and surrounded by people and life circumstances that make him (or her) uniquely who he is. And every one of us has talents, special skills, and qualities that add to that uniqueness. Even brothers and sisters who grow up in the same house with the same set of parents are very different from one another. I even believe that while cloning can make a duplicate, it is not an exact replica. Because over time, the second individual will have different experiences or influences that make him or her a distinctly unique person.

However, we sometimes take our gifts or talents for granted, or we do not even recognize them anymore. They are so easy for us that we think everyone else must have them as well. But if you ask three of your closest colleagues or friends what they consider to be your strengths, you will be surprised by how often they arrive at the same or a similar list of qualities. Your strengths will naturally come to light during your interactions with others.

I love to be in front of a crowd. When I was in fifth grade, I would write plays to present before our class with my friends. They were stories with comedic theatrics, and a bit of drama blended in. My teachers were amazed that I could pull off these productions and cause my fellow classmates to roar with laughter. Later, in high school and college, I would quickly become the lead speaker in any given classroom presentation or team interaction. I had no trouble speaking up in class. Even in my adult life, getting before a big crowd at a convention, or giving a formal presentation to a city council—I am quite comfortable. I do not understand how public speaking is one of the top rated fears for adults because it is something I love to do. Others have confirmed that it is definitely one of my skill sets, and I am often invited to speak at professional meetings and conferences. And get paid to do it!

You have your own set of skills. What are those skills that make you unique or that your friends often compliment you on? Are you great at cooking or hosting parties? Is teaching children a gift for you? Do you spend weekends studying or reading history because that's a passion? Are you great at fixing anything mechanical? Be more attuned to what you bring to the table...it can often support the attainment of your dreams. Don't limit yourself...you can be really good in many areas...list a few of your attributes. We sometimes take our strengths for granted or cannot easily identify them. Ask a trusted friend or family member what he or she thinks are your strengths and list them below:

I am good at:

_____

_____

_____

_____

_____

_____

My friends, family, or others have told me that I'm good at:

_____

_____

_____

_____

_____

_____

_____

What activities or experiences were you passionate about when you were younger? How do they relate to what you dream about having now? How have those passions changed or developed? Can you dare to be passionate again? If you had a chance to do something that would support your passion, what would it be?

_____

_____

_____

_____

_____

_____

_____

Now, look at those lists. Are you using those talents or skill sets today? In your job? In your life? If not, why not? It is time to start looking at your passions to see how they can be a greater part of your life.

Is the Time Right?

Sometimes, people will give as an excuse that the timing is bad to start working toward the life of their dreams. When my husband and I opened our wine tasting room in Old Town, the country was in the middle of a deep recession. My employer was talking about layoffs, and employees were taking pay cuts. Opening a new business was a very scary step. But we had confidence in ourselves, our product, and our abilities. And we knew that failing was not an option...we were going to work and market like crazy to make it work. If we had not opened our shop when the unique opportunity presented itself, we would not have built such a successful business. There is never a bad time; there are just better times or different ways to push forward.

So look at the timing of your goal or dreams...if not now, when? If you found out that you only had one more year to live, would you say, "Forget bad timing; let's just do it!" That's the approach that you might want to take. Are you waiting for something? To pay off your mortgage? To get married? To get divorced? For your kids to grow older or move out? To make enough money? To be retired? Maybe the timing is to take smaller steps toward your Dream Life...biding your time until you can take bigger leaps. As long as you are moving forward, the time is always good to create the life of your dreams.

So, what's stopping you? Have you identified the reasons why you are not pursuing your dream? Have you written them down? Looked at them? Now is the time to determine whether there is a way around or over your obstacles. Can you ask for help? Is there someone you can meet who has faced similar issues, or can be supportive to your goals? You don't have to have all the answers now... but what are some steps you can take to start overcoming your obstacles?

_____

_____

_____

_____

_____

_____

_____

_____

_____

The timing is now. If you wait, then you will be in this same place years from now wishing that you had made a move forward. There has got to be a way...find it, and start moving toward your dream.

The story of "The Daffodil Principle" originally appeared nearly ten years ago in Jaroldeen Edwards' book *Celebration!* It demonstrates the principle of moving forward in steps, incrementally over time, and what an impact those small efforts can make. The story begins with an adult daughter telling her mother that they need to go see the daffodils before they stop blooming. The mother is reluctant and doesn't want to waste time driving out to see some flowers. Her daughter insists and says they will regret it if they do not see them. So they go. They park near a small church and walk down the path. When they turn the corner, the mother gasps at the sight before her. Five acres are filled with the most beautiful flowers she has ever seen. When the mother asks who planted all of these flowers, the daughter replies that it was one woman who lives in a simple home nearby. When they walk up to the home, there is a poster out front that reads:

Answers to the Questions I Know You Are Asking

50,000 bulbs

One at a time

By one woman

2 hands, 2 feet

and very little brain

Began in 1958

The mother comments to her daughter that she is amazed how one woman, planting one bulb at a time, over the course of time, made such an incredible difference. Then she reflects on how sad she is about her own life, and how she wishes she had started such a goal many years ago. Her daughter looks at her and wisely says, "Start Today."

There is no time like the present...make a choice to move forward.

Chapter 2 Highlights:
Defining Your Passion

Stepping out is what a horse does when it starts to move forward in confidence and grace. What are you doing to step out toward your own passion?

◊ Is this where you want to be?

◊ What do you love doing, and are you doing it now?

◊ What are your gifts? Are you using them?

◊ What is missing, and what do you want to do more of?

Chapter 3

Saying the Dream Out Loud

*"Everything becomes a little different as soon
as it is spoken out loud."*
Hermann Hesse, Nobel Price for Literature

Talk about it. You need to say your dream out loud. This makes it real and no longer a fantasy. Once you have defined your Dream Life and committed yourself to achieving it, start talking about it! Talking about your goals makes them emotionally real. It allows people to help you reach your goal and support you along the way.

Saying something out loud is powerful. And it can be scary and risky too. People will notice. They will start to hold you accountable. Be prepared that some people may criticize or undermine you. Don't worry about it—this is your dream, not anyone else's dream.

As I told you earlier and it bears repeating here, before we had our ranch and winery, we already had the name chosen—"Hacienda de las Rosas," which translates to "Big House of the Roses." When I would tell people about our dream, they would ask, "Where is your ranch?" And I would point to my head and say, "It's right here, but one day, it will be real." Years later, when I drove up to the Spanish adobe home with the rose garden and large land for horses, I knew we had found our dream home and property. We recognized it because we had already defined it and said it out loud.

Thinking It First...Intentional Thoughts

The movie and book, *The Secret*, created by Australian Rhonda Byrne, defines "the Secret" as the "Law of Attraction," meaning the principle that "like attracts like." Byrne states, "What we do is we attract into our lives the things we want, and that is based on what we're thinking and feeling." The principle explains that we create our own circumstances by the choices we make in life. And the choices we make are fueled by our thoughts—which means our thoughts are very powerful.

You are putting out thoughts—consciously and unconsciously. Saying those thoughts out loud in a positive manner is very important. Sometimes, people will focus on how it is. A person will describe his or her current reality—"I'm in debt. I'm overweight. I'll never have a great relationship." However, the more you think about and focus on the current situation, the more you attract that situation—you will continue to be in debt, or overweight, or in a bad relationship.

The famous race car driver Mario Andretti once shared that one of the key successes of being a driver is not to look at the wall. Your hands and thoughts will follow your eyes. He cautioned that staring at the wall will actually pull you toward it—exactly where you do not want to go when travelling at high speeds! The idea is to focus on the inside curve of the track and the ultimate finish line. With this type of focus, Andretti took 109 career wins on major circuits, including the Indianapolis 500 (1969), Daytona 500 (1967), and the Formula One World Championship.

After learning this key message, my husband and I changed our "talk" into more positive, uplifting messages and talk. For instance, we transformed the statement "We are in debt" into "We are debt demolishers." And we soon became debt demolishers! We took all our debt, put it on a spreadsheet, and carefully tracked how much we paid down each month. Some months, it barely moved. Other months, we would see hundreds of dollars shaved off. We worked hard and took the steps to start reducing and then demolishing our business and credit card debts. It may seem like a small word change, but thinking and saying that we are demolishing the debt is a much more powerful thought and statement.

Think of what you want to achieve and put it into words. Words are very powerful. The old adage of "Sticks and stones may break my bones, but words can never hurt me" is not true at all. We all heal from physical hurts of the past, but we can quickly recall hurtful words that were said to us, even if they were said many years ago. The same goes for positive words. If you have a parent, teacher, coach, or friend tell you something positive about yourself...you often remember those words as well. Putting your thoughts, passions, and goals into positive words is very powerful.

Think of what you want to achieve and put it into words:

_____

_____

_____

_____

_____

_____

Do not worry about the "how." You will figure that out later. The goal here is to put your dream into words and to say it out loud.

Faking It Until You Make It

Anyone who has ever gone to the movies is aware of and appreciates the works of Steven Spielberg. As a director, Spielberg has produced and directed some of the top moneymaking and award-winning movies of all time, including *Jaws, Schindler's List, E.T.,* and the Indiana Jones film series. However, Steven didn't just land into movies. He is definitely a self-made man who had a dream long before his current success. When he was a boy, he would run around school with his 8mm camera, filming live action scenes. By the time he was twelve, he had already envisioned receiving an Oscar and had begun rehearsing his acceptance speech. When he finished high school, he took a tour of Universal Studios and met the head of the studio, who took a liking to him and invited Spielberg to come by and see him at the studio. The very next day, Spielberg showed up at the lot, wearing a suit and tie and carrying his dad's briefcase with a lunch. The guard assumed that he worked at the studio and waved him in through the gate and onto the studio lot. Spielberg soon became a regular fixture on the lot, learning from directors and making lunch appointments with famous actors like Cary Grant. He eventually found an empty office, bought his own nameplate, and set up shop. At the age of twenty-eight, Spielberg made the movie *Jaws*, the highest grossing film to date at the time. He literally acted like he belonged at the studio, and he finally proved and earned the right to be there.

Skype is another billion dollar company that started with a dream. The service allows users to communicate with peers by voice using a microphone, video by using a webcam, and instant messaging over the Internet. Skype was first released in 2003 and written by Estonian developers Arpit Gupta, Priit Kasesalu, and Jaan Tallinn. It developed into a platform with over 600 million users and was bought by Microsoft in 2011 for $8.5 billion. During Skype's early days, "we faked a lot of it," says Eileen Burbidge, one of the early employees. Before launching SkypeOut, for example, the team stayed up all night with spreadsheets trying to figure out what country to country landline charges should be. Rather than push back the launch date, Burbidge said, they ended up just making it up. "Now, obviously, that's a little bit foolhardy—I wouldn't recommend anybody do this—but my point is, we didn't over-analyze."

The first time my husband and I attended a horse show for the Peruvian Paso Horse, we were in awe of the gorgeous horses and the trappings of the show atmosphere. Most large ranches have large trucks and horse trailers, fancy stable decorations, and professional trainers and workers who clean the stalls and prepare the horses for the show. We couldn't afford those types of trappings since we handled our own transportation, and we cleaned, fed, and watered our own horse. We entered our one and only horse in the junior classes, ridden by our daughter, to get started in the show circuit.

We faked it until we made it. With only one horse, we dressed up our stall area with fancy show curtains that I bought on eBay, and we brought our patio furniture to create a picnic area. We made our area look just as good as any of the millionaire ranches' areas, and we got compliments, and made friends. Did we take home the blue ribbon? Not at first. But we worked at it, hired a trainer to work with us at our ranch, and eventually, we took home some awards. And we had fun in the process. Those horse shows were a lot of hard work, and we were often dirty and tired at the end of the day, but it was a dream of ours to show our horses. Later, we started a national breed promotion campaign. I became President of the Southern California Peruvian Paso Horse Club and was elected as a board member of the newly established breed national organization. That was a long way from having a junior rider on a single horse for our ranch.

Faking it until you make it is not about being insincere. It is not about being a fake person. It's about being courageous and committed to pursuing your dream. Almost every successful person has moments of insecurity, but sometimes, you need to act confident when you don't feel confident. Be confident to move forward...to introduce yourself, to get out there where you need to be, to stretch yourself outside of your comfort zone.

Living "As If" to Build Your Confidence

The next step is to start living "as if" you have already achieved your goals. For instance, if your goal is to lose forty pounds and run a half-marathon, then you should throw out all fattening food from the house and only have a fridge filled with healthy choices. You will create a schedule where running on a regular basis is already part of your daily or weekly ritual. You will purchase the shoes and clothes needed for your runs, and you will go ahead and register for the half-marathon, even if you aren't ready yet! And you will tell people of your plans. Then, not only will the dream start to become more real, but because you said it out loud, you are now more accountable.

If you want to have a better job, then you should already be working on your resume, even if there is not a job in sight. You will start building your profile and network on social media. At your current position, you will continue to strive to do an even better job to hone additional skills or have a great reputation in your current environment. Dress a step up to look more professional and be taken more seriously. You will start letting your friends and colleagues know about your goals. By doing so, your intentional words and thinking will help you gain exposure to new break-through ideas.

You must have faith in yourself. By pursuing your dream, you are placing a bet on yourself. Fear and indecision can go hand-in-hand when considering self-confidence. Even the bravest, most courageous people can face a lack of confidence. But the difference is that they push forward...having faith in themselves.

Webster's Dictionary defines self-confidence as "confidence in oneself and in one's powers and abilities," which means that you are completely in control. It's not what someone else thinks...it's what you think and believe about yourself. When we started our winery, we did not have a background in viticulture, nor a long family history of wine-making, but we figured that if other people could do it, then why not us? Have we had moments of insecurity? Of course! But we push through them, or learn new skills, or find out whether someone can help us. And success helps build more confidence. But at some point, you are the one to make the decision to move forward and take that step...it's all up to you.

As a longtime supervisor, I have had many people come to me for advice. Some would ask whether they should go back to school and obtain their master's degrees or whether they should move to a new job in another department. We would always talk about the pros and cons, and then my final advice would be "The whole world will tell you, 'No'...Tell yourself, 'YES' and just go for it!"

I just read an interesting article about Barbara Corcoran, the successful real estate mogul and *Shark Tank* television star. She stated that she owed her success to her own insecurity. "I have to prove that I am not stupid. Without that insecurity, I don't think I could have ever built the business I did. I don't think I would work as hard." So despite her insecurities, she pushed herself to just do it. She said that with every door she pushed through, she was scared and uncertain, but she was committed to proving she could do it. And she shared that, amazingly, she always found she could accomplish what she set out to achieve. If you don't give yourself permission or the "go" signal, then who will?

The dream can be in your head, but you have to say it out loud to start making it real.

Chapter 3 Highlights:

Saying the Dream Out Loud

Neigh **is the vocal sound a horse makes when communicating to humans or other horses. Make sure to vocalize your dream to others as well.**

◊ What is your dream and have you put it into words?

◊ Tell a supportive friend or relative.

◊ What can you do that provides a tangible step toward your dream?

◊ How can you start to "fake it" by living as if you are already in the dream life?

Chapter 4

What's Stopping You?

"Nothing is predestined: The obstacles of your past can become the gateways that lead to new beginnings."
Ralph Blum, writer and cultural anthropologist

Fear is the biggest destroyer of dreams. Fear of the unknown, fear of change, fear of failure, fear of embarrassment, fear of risk. Surprisingly, even fear of success can be a real fear.

Sean Stephenson is an amazing man. Fear has never stopped him. He was born with osteogenesis imperfecta, a disease where the bones in the body are so brittle and weak that they break easily. When he was born, the ordeal of the birth process broke most of the bones in his tiny baby body, and for weeks, he was left to heal in an incubator. Doctors told his parents that he would not have long to live. However, his parents refused to believe in his inability to survive and began to take measures to keep their son alive and healthy. In a crucial moment of his young life, he was dressed and ready to go out trick-or-treating with friends. He was excitedly rolling around on the floor when his leg caught on the coffee table and the impact broke his leg. With Sean screaming in pain, his mother rushed to his side. There was no taking him to the hospital since the doctors could not do anything. He would literally have to lie in that same place and not be moved for some time to allow the bone to heal and set. His mother soothed him, and she tried to distract him with games they often played. However, he was not having any of it, and at one point, in pain and frustration, he cried out, "WHY ME?" Then his mother made a statement that impacted the rest of his life. She asked him whether this situation was going to limit him for the rest of his life. In his book *Get Off Your 'But': How to End Self-Sabotage and Stand Up for Yourself,* Sean shares how fear and the "buts" in your life can stop you from achieving your dream. At that moment of his mom's comment, he decided that he wasn't going to let his illness hold him back. Today, Sean is a successful author and nationally recognized speaker with a loving wife and rich life. Not bad for a guy who was not supposed to live more than a few days past birth.

What are your fears? What is stopping you? Are you afraid of failure...afraid of success...afraid of what others will think? It's time to identify those "buts" or "fears" in your life that keep you from moving forward. For instance, if you are overweight and you have failed at diets many times, what is really stopping you from losing that weight as you desire? If you always wanted to open that hair salon or pet store, what is stopping you? If you are an artist and want to get your artwork out into the world, what is preventing you from making that a priority in your life? If you want to work for yourself, what steps are you taking to own your own business or franchise?

This discussion is just for you...to get in touch with those fears or "buts." What's holding you back? Write down your fears and identify them. They aren't right or wrong. However, they are very real, and you need to get a sense of what they are.

If you aren't following your dream, why not?

_____

_____

_____

_____

Do you have a physical or mental disability that you believe is holding you back?

_____

_____

_____

_____

Do you have people around you who have certain expectations, or do you have responsibilities to others that take priority over your own goals?

_____

_____

_____

_____

Do you lack something...skills...money...resources? What are they?

_____

_____

_____

_____

Does your goal seem completely unattainable...why?

_____

_____

_____

_____

This list is for you. The fears or "buts" in your life are what are holding you back. If you want to move forward, you need to identify and deal with these obstacles. Identifying them is the first part of the process.

Who Cares What Other People Think?

My husband and I have a good friend, Tom McCutchan, who was part of the first Navy Seal squad and saw action in the Vietnam War. When we first met him, he was running a successful real estate office. He is a person of integrity—a straight shooter, who tells it like it is. He shared with us his philosophy in dealing with various people in a somewhat drama-filled real estate industry: "What other people think about me is none of my business." The "other people" he is referring to are the naysayers, the gossipers, the people who want to drag you down. He said, "I don't have time for those people, and I'm going to live my life the way that I see fit." Tom has led a successful life as a businessperson, and now he is living a wonderful retirement of traveling and fishing with his wife, Vicki. Tom and Vicki have an amazingly positive life, filled with friends, family, and gratitude...they waste no time on what others think about their life or their choices...what a powerful life position.

Many of us can go back through our lives and think of all the times when someone else's opinion of us either stopped us from doing something or caused us to do something we didn't really want to do. Kids are particularly vulnerable to this type of feedback. As a result, they will unfortunately make life decisions based on ridicule or advice they received at a young age. For instance, I grew very tall early in life, so I was made fun of for my height and towering stature in middle school. It didn't help that I also had bright red carrot-top frizzy hair. The result was that I tended to hunch down or wear only flat shoes to minimize any height advantage during those years. During this gangly tall period in middle school, I never thought I was particularly attractive. Being a tomboy didn't help with being as "girlie" as the other girls. Several people would make fun of my height, or shoe size, or frizzy red hair and freckles. I just didn't think that it was in my future to be attractive. Over the years, when someone told me I looked beautiful or complimented my appearance, I would just think the person was being polite. Finally, after all these years, I have come to appreciate my own look. I love being tall…I like my red hair and fading freckles. Do I look like a model—heck no! At least not one whom I know, but I am comfortable in my own skin. It's unfortunate that it took me so long to reach this position because of comments made to me almost thirty years ago.

One of the most famous basketball coaches in UCLA's history was John Wooden, who inspired players to their best efforts through his leadership and coaching skills. In his book *The Essential Wooden*, he states, "Outsiders will look to the won-loss ratio (in whatever forms) to ascertain what you have achieved and whether you deserve to be called a 'success.' But ultimately the only person who can truly give a valid appraisal of personal success is the individual himself or herself—you for you; me for me." Much attention is given to UCLA's seven consecutive championships and eighty-eight consecutive game-winning streak. However, in his book, Wooden mentions that earlier successes in 1964 and 1965 meant so much more to him. With an antiquated facility, and the odds stacked against them during those early days, he notes that he himself knew his team and program was successful, before the later, more widely acclaimed achievements.

There are sometimes words or messages that are said about you in the past that you never forget and now shape your image of you. Think back to when you were young. Were you told by an adult that there was something you could not do? Were you told that you weren't good at math, that you'd never be able to play the piano, that you have no sense of direction? Were you put down for your accent, your hair color, your height, your skin color, or your weight? What message was shared with you that you can still hear today in your mind? Has it imprinted itself on your brain so that you believe it yourself? Sometimes, we don't even realize that these other people's opinions are holding us back or keeping us from achieving our dreams.

When Stephen King submitted his iconic thriller *Carrie* for publication, he received thirty rejections, finally causing King to give up and throw the manuscript in the trash. However, his wife had faith in his dream; she took the book out of the garbage and encouraged him to resubmit it. King now has dozens of books published with the distinction of being one of the best-selling authors of all time. His wife's words of encouragement made a huge difference. Sometimes, it takes someone who believes in you to help you believe in yourself.

Think back to the last time someone shared his (or her) opinion of you. What did he say? How did it make you feel? Did you agree with him? Did it make you stop doing something or start doing it differently? If it's just someone else's opinion, maybe it is none of your business. Maybe it's just that...his or her opinion. That doesn't make it fact. It doesn't make it right. It takes no qualifications to be a critic...aim higher and be the star!

Stop Wasting Time

Despite all the advances of the modern world, I believe we waste too much time on electronics and the latest wizardry...it literally can suck hours out of your day! Think how much time is spent on the computer mindlessly searching through the Internet, or getting involved in chat rooms with folks you don't know, nor will ever meet. How much time is spent on texting, tweeting, and emailing?

And television—how many reality shows can possibly be watched in any given day? My feeling about reality television is that I would rather live my own reality than watch someone else's! The happiest people watch less than one hour of television a day, according to a study of 40,000 people who took *National Geographic*'s True Happiness Test. It seems that more happiness is gained by being with family and friends or engaging in an enjoyable hobby or activity. Television—both advertising and programming—is designed to make us want things and to feel less satisfied with what we have.

I understand that we live in a consumerism world and technology is firmly part of our lives—I get that. However, do we need to stay connected and involved every moment of the day? I was boarding a plane yesterday for a forty-minute flight when the man in front of me asked whether there was WIFI available. This was an older plane, so the flight attendant responded that it was not available. This man was very upset with the answer, but I thought to myself, "You can't disconnect from the world for forty minutes?"

There should be a limit to the amount of time one spends with a device—computer, phone, or television—rather than living your life. Do you really need a television in every room of the house? Think of how many minutes and hours of your own day are spent wasting time watching television, playing video games, and on mindless computer searches. At the end of your life, are you going to wish that you watched that reality show? Are you going to be glad that you read and answered every single email? Or would it be more important to spend some time with your teenager? Or go out to dinner with a friend you haven't seen in a while? Or take the time to have a date with your spouse? Or go back to school, take that dance class, go fishing, start writing that book…the list is endless. Which of these will have greater impact and be remembered more—living your life or wasting your life?

Five years ago, my husband and I completely quit the television habit. We cancelled our cable service and literally did not watch television for almost two years. At first, it was hard. We had certain programs we had watched which we were no longer able to, and events were missed, like Sunday afternoon football games. However, over time, we started not to miss them anymore. Instead, we filled the time on things that we wanted to do, and we spent time building our business and working on our Dream Life. Not watching television actually freed up hours during the day. And another side benefit—it took a lot of negativity out of our home life. Most news programs are filled with bad news, and most reality shows can be filled with drama…and that was now gone. Instead of dwelling on a recent shooting or what a Hollywood star was doing that week, we were living our own life. While it's good to be informed, there's not much we could do about solving many of the bad news stories. Why let so much negativity enter your home? Some of our friends can't believe that we don't have television, but it has been very freeing. We recently started having Netflix movies delivered, and it is fun to watch a movie now and then for entertainment. However, after it is done, the television goes off and we are back to living life again.

What are your time wasters? What activities do you participate in that add no real value other than to kill time? Do you lose hours a day to these activities, and what would you rather be doing? Or do you procrastinate or do something to take time away from working on tasks that could help move you toward your goals? I tend to start cleaning when I don't want to work on a particular project. The kitchen and bathrooms get scrubbed and laundry gets done, but I don't get much further on that project that really is on my "to do" list. I must have passed this on to my daughter because she would often put off studying for finals to clean her room instead. She had an amazingly organized closet! She would eventually study through the night and had really good grades, but missed out on a lot of sleep during those teenage years.

For the course of one week, I encourage you to monitor and document the time you spend watching television, playing video games, mindless Internet searching, chat room discussions, texting, tweeting, and emailing. Keep track of those times where you should be focusing on your action items to move you toward the Dream Life, but you like to meander into other activities that take you away from those tasks. I think you will be amazed by the time spent (or maybe wasted) on these activities. The first step is identifying the wasteful time, and the only way to do that is to track it. I'm not suggesting that all of this time is wasteful...we obviously need the computer and Internet for work and some of our social life, but the amount of time on the computer should be spent toward achieving the Dream Life you hope to live.

For the next seven days, just for your own knowledge, track your computer, phone, and television activities. Once you have identified the number of minutes and hours spent per day, the next step is to redirect some of that time toward something more productive, enlightening, or toward achieving your Dream Life.

Daily Tracking Form — Where are your Time Wasters?

Sunday	Hours/Mins
Computer	
Television	
Games	
Social Media/Texting/Tweeting	
Intentional Procrastination Activity	
Other _____	

Monday	Hours/Mins
Computer	
Television	
Games	
Social Media/Texting/Tweeting	
Intentional Procrastination Activity	
Other _____	

Tuesday	Hours/Mins
Computer	
Television	
Games	
Social Media/Texting/Tweeting	
Intentional Procrastination Activity	
Other _____	

Wednesday	Hours/Mins
Computer	
Television	
Games	
Social Media/Texting/Tweeting	
Intentional Procrastination Activity	
Other _____	

Thursday	Hours/Mins
Computer	
Television	
Games	
Social Media/Texting/Tweeting	
Intentional Procrastination Activity	
Other _____	

Friday	Hours/Mins
Computer	
Television	
Games	
Social Media/Texting/Tweeting	
Intentional Procrastination Activity	
Other _____	

Saturday	Hours/Mins
Computer	
Television	
Games	
Social Media/Texting/Tweeting	
Intentional Procrastination Activity	
Other _____	

Overcoming the Past

We all have something—something in our pasts that has either made us who we are, or has given us the insecurities or fears that we have today. You might have been raised in a very poor family, had little family structure, been raised by a grandparent or in a foster home. You might have been abused by someone whom you trusted or had things stolen from you. You might have been passed over for deserved promotions or laid off. You might have a child with a health issue or learning disability. You might have just found out you have cancer or another life-threatening illness. We all have something.

Many successful people in the world have overcome extreme adversity. Fitness guru and television pitch man Tony Little has experienced a few setbacks—struck by lightning (twice), dad committed suicide, drugged and kidnapped by a predator, car accidents, and recently, his twins were born prematurely. In his book, *There's Always a Way*, he states, "I figured we all have adversities in our life, but if we change our mindsets on the adversities, they can end up becoming victories. I went through years of tragedy and adversity, but that always seemed to parallel with a later victory. It made me think how the power of the mind is amazing in business, entrepreneurship, and success—and maybe it's not so complicated." Here is a list of some other folks who had a few setbacks before their ultimate success:

Oprah Winfrey: Oprah faced a hard road to get to her current position, enduring an often abusive childhood as well as numerous career setbacks including being fired from her job as a television reporter because she was "unfit for television." After creating her own show and media empire, today she is one of the richest and most successful businesspeople in the world.

Bethany Hamilton: A natural surfer, Bethany began competing professionally as a young child. However, at age thirteen, she lost her arm and nearly lost her life in a vicious shark attack. One month later, she was back on her surfboard with a determined spirit and positive attitude. Two years later, she won first place in the Explorer Women's Division of the NSSA National Championships. Her story was made into the inspiring major motion picture *Soul Surfer.*

Stephen Hawking: One of the most brilliant scientific minds on the planet, Hawking has contributed groundbreaking work in the areas of physics and cosmology. He has written a number of books—including the bestselling *A Brief History of Time*—that helps to explain some of the world's biggest mysteries. Hawking has done all of this despite being diagnosed at age twenty-one with amyotrophic lateral sclerosis, aka ALS or Lou Gehrig's disease, a disorder that includes weakness and muscle atrophy. Now in his seventies, Hawking is almost entirely paralyzed and must communicate using a device that can generate speech. He has three children, one of whom has written three children's books with him.

Melissa Stockwell: Stockwell is a war veteran with the U.S. Army, a Purple Heart recipient, a paralympian, a paratriathlete, and an above-the-knee amputee. In 2004, she lost her leg when a roadside bomb exploded during a convoy. A diver in high school, she began to swim at Walter Reed Hospital as part of her physical therapy. She eventually competed in the 2008 Paralympic Games for the U.S. team, becoming the record holder for the 100 meter butterfly and the 100 meter freestyle.

Michael Jordan: A man often lauded as the best basketball player of all time, Jordan was actually cut from his high school basketball team. Luckily, Jordan didn't let this setback stop him from playing the game. He has stated, "I have missed more than 9,000 shots in my career. I have lost almost 300 games. On 26 occasions I have been entrusted to take the game winning shot, and I missed. I have failed over and over and over again in my life. And that is why I succeed."

Search the Internet and you will find literally hundreds of stories of successful people with very real problems who overcame adversity. In their own individual ways, they have each made a difference, excelling in their fields and achieving their life goals. We all have something...in our past or our current lives...that is holding us back. It's time to start moving past it.

Chapter 4 Highlights:
What's Stopping You?

Spooky describes a horse that is easily frightened and shies or runs away from imagined danger. What is scaring you from going toward your goals in your own life?

◊ Identify what is stopping you.

◊ Is the obstacle internal or external? Is there a way around it?

◊ What are your time wasters?

◊ Is there something in your past that has held you back?

Chapter 5

Making a Plan for the Dream Life

"Our goals can only be reached through a vehicle of a plan, in which we must fervently believe, and upon which we must vigorously act. There is no other route to success."
Pablo Picasso

Why are you doing all the things you do on a day in and day out basis? Why do you get up early to get ready for work? Why do you travel through traffic-filled streets to get to that job? Why do you spend 8-10 hours at that job? How do you spend your free time—what do you do then? The real question behind all these questions is "*Why* do you do what you do?" If the answer is "To pay the rent or mortgage" or "Because that's what a grownup does in this world," that probably isn't a great goal for your life. So, you might want to ask yourself, "What do I really want?" What do I want my life to look like? What kind of house will I live in? What kind of friends do I want? What kind of person do I want to be? Does my current life reflect the type of life that I want?" "Is this the life that I want for my family?" In other words, if you were looking at a photo of your Dream Life…what would it look like? Now compare that photo to your current life…how does it compare?

In *The 7 Habits of Highly Effective People*, bestselling author Stephen Covey says that Habit 2 is to "Begin with the End in Mind." He shares that you must summon the ability to envision in your mind what you cannot presently see with your eyes. Make a conscious effort to visualize who you are and what you want in life; otherwise, you empower other people and circumstances to shape you and your life by default. He states, "Begin with the End in Mind means to begin each day, task, or project with a clear vision of your desired direction and destination, and then continue by flexing your proactive muscles to make things happen." When my husband is making a wine, he is already thinking about the end in mind—the color, the taste, the complexity of the final product…and then works backwards to create the process to make that particular wine. In horse breeding…before the baby horse is born, a responsible breeder thinks of the end in mind. What kind of conformation is desired, what personality, color, or temperament should be in that new foal? The breeder will identify a mare and stallion to create the dream horse…the end is in mind before the breeding process starts.

For many years, I worked for a city government, starting as an administrative trainee, and within eight years, became a deputy director…a huge leap across several classifications. My ultimate goal was to be a department director. After working in management for several years, I was appointed as head of a department. I had finally made it! However, my days were long and the stress was high. Every day was filled with meetings, emergencies—both real and imagined—personnel issues, and the bureaucracy of paperwork. I worked hard and strived to be the best person in the job. And I was rewarded…with more work…more problems to solve… more emergencies to handle. It's funny that when an organization finds you are a problem solver, you are rewarded with lots more problems to solve!

Always wanting to stretch myself, my new goal was to earn the job above me. A new administration came in, and due to frequent turnover in management, I had ten bosses in three years. With each new boss, I would try to prove myself and take on more work. But that boss would leave or get moved, and I'd have to repeat the same process with the next new person. When it was time to fill the position above me, I truly felt I was the most qualified. Many peers from across the organization assured me that the job would be mine. However, the position was filled by a friend and former colleague of one of the top managers. Instead of saying, "The heck with this; I'm not happy and I'm going to find something else," I stayed and worked only harder. I took on more responsibilities, worked longer hours, and tried to be the "can-do" person for everybody. It became an endless cycle. That new boss left the City after nine months, and I felt for sure my time had come.

After he left, the City was faced with several large emergencies, including the Witch Creek Fires that swept across San Diego. I took on the role of Emergency Operations Logistics Chief and worked long days and weeks to meet all the needs for that emergency. I acted in that additional role for almost six months, and I thought my superiors surely could see I deserved the job. However, the new CFO wanted "new blood" and hired another man from outside the organization. The insult was that they also paid him $20,000 more in salary than me, the person who had been doing two jobs for the organization during the past six months! That was the final straw and insult for me.

I ended up moving to another department for six months to plan my next steps. I decided that I could no longer be part of an organization that did not appreciate my efforts and hard work, nor part of a team that did not support its members. And I wanted some freedom…from the daily grind of waking up, driving an hour to and from work, being stressed, always handling problems, and not being appreciated. I wanted more time for me, for my family, and to pursue my dream.

I did a lot of soul searching during that time, and I asked myself, "What do I *really* want? If I'm going to work this hard and place so much energy into my work, without anything in return, then why am I doing it?" And I found that it no longer was a particular role or title that I wanted. I had worked too hard for that goal. I had almost made myself sick with stress trying to get that "title." But now I didn't really want that at all. And I was tired of working for bosses who had disappointed me, time and again. What I really wanted was "freedom." We all have our definition of freedom, and for me, freedom means I can choose the projects I want to work on. It means I can work the hours I want and take off the hours I want. It means I have money in the bank, my bills can be paid, and I don't have to worry at night about not having enough. It means I can spend time with those who are most important to me. I can take the time to enjoy moments with my kids. I hadn't had that time when they were little, but I would love to do it now that they were young adults and had become really cool people to hang out with. I could travel with my husband or have the time or resources to go spend more time with my parents in their later years. It meant doing work that had meaning for me and allowed me to follow my strengths and passions.

What was the price tag for this freedom? Well, my husband and decided that freedom can only come from various sources. First, we need money. Money to buy our freedom. This would pay all the bills...take care of our debt...help us expand our family businesses...pay for vacations...and would be available to help our kids and others. The goal isn't the money—it's the freedom. The money was the means to help purchase the freedom...almost like a price tag.

Second, we wanted to work for ourselves and not be beholden to another person or company's vision. I wanted to give up having a boss who decided what the priorities were and where I had to spend my time each day. If we had to work, then we both wanted to do something we enjoyed, to pay for the freedom.

And finally, we wanted to have time. Time to participate in activities that we both enjoyed like horse shows or short vacation trips. Time to spend with our kids or family, and time to just sit on the back porch and enjoy the sunset. Time is such a precious commodity. I've always strived to fill every moment of the day with activity. Why not make those moments consumed with activities I want to do, rather than have to do.

What's your ultimate Dream Life? Why do you do what you do? Why do you work? Why do you get out of bed? What is the Dream

Life you would like to achieve? Write down some ideas for your own Dream Life:

_____

_____

_____

_____

_____

_____

_____

_____

_____

Making It Real

Once you have the idea for your Dream Life, write it down! In fact, write it where you can see it every day. Put it on your computer screen, your whiteboard, at the top of your day planner, or on your phone. You need to keep it always in front of you...keep it in sight. It's amazing what the unconscious mind can do when positive influences surround it. Your mind, both conscious and unconscious, will see that message written in clear view. And it makes it easier to make decisions that guide you to the Dream Life. For instance, if you need to purchase something, does it support your goal? If you see an opportunity, should you take it to support your goal? Are there people in your life who help to support you toward that goal? And just as important, are there things or people in your life that keep you from your goal?

Unless you win the lottery or inherit a huge sum of money, like most of us, you have to work toward your goals. What you want is usually not given to you. Making daily decisions leads you to your goal. It is never one big jump. It is a series of "baby steps" to help your achieve the Dream Life. This lesson is represented in the film *What About Bob?*, a 1991 comedy directed by Frank Oz and starring Bill Murray and Richard Dreyfuss. Murray plays Bob Wiley, a multiphobic psychiatric patient who follows his successful and egotistical psychiatrist Dr. Leo Marvin (played by Dreyfuss) on vacation. The film relates to goal setting because Dr. Marvin has just written a book called *Baby Steps*, which helps patients by instructing them to take just a few steps toward their goals...not necessarily looking for the cure right away. So for the agoraphobic Wiley, a baby step would be to open the door and take a few steps outside his apartment. The next baby step would be to get outside of the complex, and so on. By the end of the movie, Wiley has gone swimming, boating, shared a vacation with Dr. Marvin's family, and ends up on a nationally televised morning show. While the movie is a fun comedy, the idea of "baby steps" toward the goal is still a valid one.

To reach a goal, it takes a plan, with defined steps or mini-goals to help you achieve the Dream Life. Making up or setting a goal is never the hard part. We've all had lots of practice every year when January 1st rolls around. The problem is committing and carrying out the steps to achieve the goal. And that requires a plan.

Most people spend more time planning their next vacation or their kids' summer schedules than they do planning their lives. Being a success, where you feel that you are achieving and living your Dream Life, takes a lot of planning. And the plan needs to be written, reviewed, modified, and always updated. Sound like work?

Sound like one more thing to take care of? Well, it is. But as the famous leadership coach and speaker Jim Rohn once said, "If you don't design your own life plan, chances are you'll fall into someone else's plan. And guess what they have planned for you? Not much." Think of the alternative. What if you didn't set a goal or make a plan? How would that work out for you? What do you think the chances of obtaining your Dream Life would be then?

At the beginning of each year, everyone gets excited about setting resolutions and goals. I like to ask people what they are hoping to achieve because I'm interested, and I also want to be supportive. One particular response really astounded me. The person told me, "My resolution is just to do the same as last year...just survive." I thought, "That's all that you want to achieve? Wow...that particular goal is the same for wildlife...they just want to survive too. Doesn't put you much higher on the food chain than other mammals." His response made me feel sad for him, thinking that he was not taking advantage of all the talents he has nor leading himself toward a higher destination for his life.

So take a look at your Dream Life. You need to create a plan to reach it. Whether it's building a business, climbing a mountain, charting the ocean...you always need a plan for a successful voyage. It's easiest when you break it down. What are the categories of your life that would help you attain the goal? Break it down into 4-5 categories. Think of categories or pillars that would support both your professional and personal life. What do you want to achieve as an individual...is that a part of the goal?

In my case, to reach the "FREEDOM" Goal, I had five categories or "pillars." They were Financial, Special Projects, Personal, Health, and Relationships. This would be the first step—create your pillars.

You need to take the time to plan. Whether it's time away by yourself, or sitting down with your life partner, you need to think about and write down the four to six pillars that will help achieve your Dream Life. Just think of your Dream Life as a house: What are the foundation pillars that would support that house? The foundation that allows that house to be the best one for you to live your life. Remember, don't worry about "How" right now. Just put those goals or pillars in writing.

Pillar 1:

_____

_____

_____

Pillar 2:

_____

_____

_____

Pillar 3:

_____

_____

_____

Pillar 4:

_____

_____

_____

Pillar 5:

_____

_____

_____

Great start! If you feel you require more pillars or categories, then go ahead a create them. Just make sure they are broad enough categories to organize your life into a plan to help achieve that Dream Life. A few focused categories and goals are better than a long list of expanded categories and goals. Try to stay focused by not creating more than seven pillars.

Thinking and visualizing is only part of the path...the next step is to start the actual execution. Patrick Snow, in his book *The Affluent Entrepreneur*, says that the majority of people can dream, and then plan, but then they fail to take the next crucial step—execute. This step is the hardest one of all. However, it is crucial and important because it requires taking your dreams and actually working the steps to make them come to fruition. The action of executing separates the "dreamers" from the "achievers." Anyone can dream. Only a few actually start the execution to achieve the dream.

After you have established your pillars, it's time to write mini-goals within each pillar to help support the Dream Life. It takes a bit of thinking, but setting your goals for the next year will help to support and move you toward your life plan by determining where you spend your time, money, and efforts.

In my case, for the Financial pillar, I had to define the exact revenue, the exact elimination for debt, the amount of money that needs to be in savings, etc. For Personal, I had specific goals I wanted to attain this year such as writing this book and getting it published. Under Relationships, I had a goal that my husband and I take a mini-vacation each quarter; that goal requires that during this quarter, we are already thinking, planning, and making reservations for the next quarter. It can't just happen...it takes planning.

To help provide an example, here are two mini-goals per pillar that I had for last year:

Pillar 1: Financial

Tasting room brings in an average of $1,000 per day, and business activities that achieve over $1 million per year.

Book four parties a month, and participate in two outside promotional events each month (which help support that revenue stream).

Pillar 2: Special Projects

Build gate and beautiful landscaped entry for new tasting room in Ramona.

Remodel kitchen and complete by Christmas.

Pillar 3: Personal

Hire and work with professional coach for six months.

Start writing book and commit to publication no later than May 2013.

Pillar 4: Health

Lose 10 lbs by June 2013.

Commit to horseback riding/walking program of three hours per week.

Pillar 5: Relationships

Take mini-vacations with husband, at least one per quarter.

Visit son in military and fly him home at least once a year for family visits.

Writing these mini-goals under your categories not only provides a path to achieving your Dream Life, but it helps you to organize your time, energy, and talents toward the goal. Without these mini-goals, you are just wandering around, hoping and wishing that your Dream Life will be reached. This ain't . You can't just click your heels and hope that you can go home to your Dream Life. You have to start making the plans and begin executing the steps.

Chapter 5 Highlights:
Making a Plan for the Dream Life

Obstacle Course – a class or race in which a horse and rider must negotiate a set of fences, which requires stamina, speed, and ability to take on unknown hurdles. Do you have a plan for your life and know what direction you are going?

◊ What is your Dream Life?

◊ Have you written it down where you see it every day?

◊ What do you want your life ultimately to look like?

◊ What are the Pillars for your plan?

◊ Have you identified the goals within those pillars?

Chapter 6

Working the Dream…Why Is It So Hard?

*"A dream doesn't become reality through magic;
it takes sweat, determination, and hard work."*
Colin Powell

There is an old saying, "If you love your job, then you'll never work a day in your life." I don't know if I completely agree with it. Loving your work will definitely make the work very satisfying and fulfilling. However, it is a bit misleading to suggest that loving what you do, or working toward your dream, will somehow eliminate the hard work. Be prepared to work—sometimes harder than you ever have in your life—if you want to achieve your Dream Life.

I love basketball. As a young woman playing on a high school team back in the late '70s, I had no real women role models in sports. There were no professional women basketball teams at that time and very few women athletes portrayed on television. So my hero was Larry Bird of the Boston Celtics. Farm boy from the country, not too quick, and kind of gawky, he became one of the best players of the day in a growing field of tough city kids entering the court. What made Larry so good? He absolutely loved the game...breathed the game...and was one of the hardest working players in the sport. As a kid, he would shoot hoops before school, play the game after school, and spend his entire summer vacation on the courts. He never stopped working on his skills—shooting, passing, dribbling equally with both hands—because he wanted to be the best. The hours he spent working on his shot as a youngster paid off in big dividends in the NBA. No other player of his era was as good or as consistent a shooter as Bird. He helped lead his team to multiple championships, and he earned almost every award an athlete can win. Even as an adult player, he was always practicing... always preparing...to live his dream of being the best. He was well-known and respected for his work ethic in a sport he loved.

When you look at your Dream Life...what are you doing to achieve it? On a daily basis? What is the groundwork you are laying...what are the steps you are taking? How much sweat equity are you putting into the dream? The work may be making connections and networking, developing a great product, taking a class or lessons to hone your skills, creating an image, or a brand or marketing effort...what have you done today?

My husband and I opened our wine tasting room in Old Town, San Diego during the middle of a recession. While I worked a full-time job, he was working the winery and installing and managing vineyards for other people. We had to run a seven-days-a-week retail operation and the horse ranch and farm, with three young adult children we were still helping to support. My husband would take the first shift of the day in the store. When I got off work at 4 p.m., I would relieve him and work until closing. Our lease and location requires that we be open seven days a week...so there was no leeway to choose one day to be closed for a day of respite. With no employees—just our kids who were in college, and a friend or two who could help—we maintained that schedule for the first year. We could not afford any additional expenses or payroll and had to stay as lean as possible to keep the shop going.

Some days were so slow that we only sold one bottle of wine in an eight-hour day...that's a loooong day! We were virtually unknown. Most people who were visiting Old Town weren't thinking about wine tasting; they were more inclined to margarita drinking! Our second year brought a part-time employee and a bit more freedom. However, we continued working every weekend—our two busiest days of the week—to pull in the money to help cover the slower days. The third year brought in a few more customers as we built our wine club and customer base, and another part-time employee was added during the busy summer months. Even today, when we aren't in the store, we are still working—managing the finances, ordering supplies, making the wine, bottling, harvesting, marketing and networking, taking care of the horses and ranch—there is always something to do when building a Dream Life!

Breaking It Down

Every Dream Life is reached by a multitude of baby steps. If you see people who seem to be overnight successes, rest assured that they took a lot of little steps consistently over time to get to the level where they are today. To break it down into a simple system, do a minimum of five action steps every day to move you toward your Dream Life. In his book, The Success Principles: How to Get from Where You Are to Where You Want to Be, author and coach Jack Canfield calls these action steps "The Rule of 5." He suggests that each day, you take five specific actions or steps toward your ultimate goal. It may be as simple as making a phone call, attending a meeting, ordering a catalog, or writing a letter. Each of these individual baby steps brings you closer to your goal.

My husband and I have a big white board in our office where we write down the five steps we must take that day to obtain our goal. Maybe it's cheating a bit because we are two people doing the five steps together, but we have the same goal for our life, so it works for us to be more synchronized. For instance, today is January 2nd, and the five steps on our board are:

1. Update 2013 goals sheet and post

2. Obtain drop shipping information to assist in expanding online store

3. Call for bottle samples to explore new options and pricing

4. Make reservations for Wine Symposium

5. Place advertisement in horse club newsletter about horse exhibition at the winery

Each one of these steps helps us move forward to the expansion of our online store and product lines to bring in additional revenue, gain knowledge about the trends and products in the current wine markets, and raise the awareness of our second wine tasting room that just opened. And each of these baby steps helps us achieve our ultimate Dream Life. Now, don't think that these five steps are the only things we do during the day. We also complete our regular chores and assignments, keep the tasting room open and running, and that particular day, I spent time on a community charity event. However, these five steps were very deliberate. They were in addition to everything else we had going on in our lives. If you aren't deliberate about taking your steps, life will take over, and you won't make progress toward your goals.

Right now, your dream may seem far away. Just think of it as an ultimate destination, like a trip to Fiji or a Mediterranean Cruise. You don't have to see the whole path to those destinations. You just need to know and believe that they are there, and take the steps toward them. Writing down and tracking five steps a day will really lead to measurable movement toward your dream.

So, now that you have your Dream Life identified, what five steps are you going to do today? What baby steps can be taken to start movement in that direction. Go ahead...write them down! And keep a daily log of all your daily steps to move forward—it gives you a tremendous sense of accomplishment and your dream doesn't get lost in the daily minutiae of everyday life.

Five Action Steps for Today

1. _____
2. _____
3. _____
4. _____
5. _____

Measuring and Tracking

The only way to know whether you are reaching your goals is to have some way to measure or track your progress. What if your goal is to be fit and healthy? Well, that's not measurable. How do you know when you reach that goal? However, the plan to lose twenty-five pounds or run a half-marathon by the end of the year...

that's measurable. Your weight loss, inches lost, and amount of time and mileage achieved in running...these are easy measurable units. You easily can track your progress, or lack thereof, to know when your goal is met. If you have a goal of making $100,000 per year and getting out of credit card debt, determine how you track that progress. Do you have a method or plan for tracking it? Are you tracking your monthly credit card outstanding balances, along with interest rates? Tracking the payments along the way? How about income...are you just relying on your salary, or are you also considering and tracking other small revenue sources throughout the year? Don't plan on waiting until the end of the year to obtain a W-2 statement—you should know your progress from one month to the next.

What if part of your Dream Life is to write a book and be a successful public speaker? How many chapters do you want to have written by the end of the month? How many pages written by the end of this week? Writing the book is part of the goal, but how many copies do you ultimately want to sell? Per year? Per month? How many speaking engagements do you want to schedule? How much revenue do you want to make? Each goal should be measurable. And once you reach a particular goal, is that it? You should want to expand that measure and continue pushing forward to greater achievement.

In our case, my husband and I track our goals—number of wine club members, average dollar online sales, revenues vs. expenditure ratios, number of positive reviews by customers, etc. We create a table that is updated each month. Then we compare these numbers from month to month. Now that we've been in business a bit longer, we compare year to year. Not only do we see trends, but we also see where slow growth or big gains occurred so we can discuss and reflect. We not only track business goals, but personal goals as well. For instance, we plan a mini-getaway each quarter, and one big vacation a year. We take the steps to ensure that a quarter doesn't go by and we suddenly realize that we did not have our intended break. Is it a perfect system? Maybe not. But it works for us.

Using this same philosophy, Google Analytics was developed as a great online system to help track the traffic and pattern of views of websites, online newsletters, and other marketing campaigns. It has the ability to share how many unique users visit your website, which pages they viewed, the average time spent on that page, whether they clicked on any links, and most importantly, how they found your website in the first place. It's a very powerful tool to see how your website is being viewed by your customers.

I'm not much of a gym person, but when I did go to the gym, the staff was big on taking measurements to help gauge one's progress. Well, I always balked at the weekly weigh-in and measuring because it was just too often for me. Since weight can sometimes plateau, I did not want to work hard all week just to be told there was no difference on the scale. So I talked my trainer into weighing and measuring me on a monthly basis instead. That system kept me motivated and wanting to continue to work hard toward my goal. Weekly measuring just didn't show enough progress for me to stay motivated. There are other people who actually want to be weighed and measured more often—sometimes daily. That system works for them and helps keep them motivated. So choose a system, or create and follow a system that works for you.

Working Hard vs. Working Your Goals

I've known a lot of hard workers. People who work two or three part-time jobs to support their families. They put in long hours and spend a good portion of their adult lives on the job. But working hard and working toward your goals are two different things. You need to be strategic. I could work my job for a boss or company for most of my life and spend lots of hours to achieve the company's goals. But is that working toward my Dream Life of Freedom? If the company goals are your Dream Life goals, then that might be the case. But the company, unless you own it, should not be in control of your whole life...you still should have some dreams of your own!

Maybe it's because I worked in government so long...over twenty years as a city employee, that I saw a lot of people just working toward retirement. In civil service, there can sometimes be a tendency to become complacent and be glad that one has a good steady government job. Don't get me wrong, I am proud of my civil service career. There were many, like me, who believed that we worked for the residents and taxpayers. We strived to be the best, saving money, creating value, and providing good customer service. However, there were those inside the organization who saw the job as a paycheck and just did their jobs. When you asked many of them what they were working for, they would reply "a good retirement." One woman would greet me with exactly how many days she had left in the workplace, such as "Hi, Tammy, only 3,405 days left until retirement." Her retirement was still several years away! Some of these individuals, as soon as they retired, came back to the City the very next week to work in a temporary capacity...in the very same cubicles and department from which they had been complaining that they wanted to be free. It was almost as if they were too afraid to leave the "nest" of work and go out and fly. Don't misunderstand me; I firmly believe in planning for your future and having a good retirement strategy. But if that's the only reason you are working, that does not seem like much of a Dream Life.

I remember attending the retirement party of a person who served the City for over thirty years. The party occurred on a Friday, and on Monday, he was back at his desk. I asked him what he was doing back...didn't he just retire? He replied, "Oh, the City will allow you to come back and work for a ninety-day provisional appointment." One day after retirement and he was already back to work in the same place he had been aching to leave all those years. It didn't make sense! He didn't have a plan. He didn't have a dream. He didn't know what to do after his job was finished. My point is that working for the sake of working, and not working toward something, isn't a life fulfilled.

Doing the Job You Have Now for the Dream of Tomorrow

Many people might read about creating the Dream Life and think, "Well, that's all well and good to have a Dream Life, but I have to pay the bills and need to take care of my kids." I get that that...boy, do I get that. My husband and I have built our winery and horse ranch, but I still had to work another "day" job to help pay for that dream. My Dream Life of Freedom was and is a work in progress. I had to work my other job for years to help support the achievement of our Dream Life. But having to work now doesn't prevent you from dreaming. Sometimes we have to do the job we have now for the dream of tomorrow.

A majority of American workers say they are unsatisfied with their jobs, and only 15.4 percent pronounce themselves "very satisfied" in their work, according to a new report by the Conference Board, a business membership and research group that has been conducting surveys about worker happiness. Older workers, in particular, have experienced the steepest drop in job satisfaction in the past twenty-five years. Why wait years to enjoy your life? Why not start doing it now, even if you still have the "day" job that pays the bills? Many paths can lead to fulfillment. While you are working the "day" job, think of ways in which you can pursue your dream or something you enjoy. If pursuing your dream is what you truly desire, then you have to make it a priority. Can you switch jobs, change fields, and start anew, or take classes to learn new skills? While you are working that job to pay the bills, can you discover ways to make old workplaces feel fresh?

As a purchasing agent, I had almost 100 people in my department who ultimately reported to me. A long-time purchasing specialist came to me with a request for projects that he could work on to expand his knowledge or take him toward an opportunity for further promotion. He felt he was "stuck" and he no longer enjoyed the work he was doing. At the time, there was a hiring freeze and positions were being cut from the City's budget, so there were limited opportunities for a traditional career move. Outside of work, this man absolutely loved to golf. His clubs resided in his car, and he played at least 2-3 times a week. All his vacations were scheduled with golf in mind.

The United States Open Tournament, otherwise known as the U.S. Open, is an annual open golf tournament, serving as the second in a series of four major championships in golf. On October

4, 2002, the United States Golf Association awarded the 2008 U.S. Open Golf Tournament to Torrey Pines Golf Course in San Diego. It was the first time the tournament would be played at Torrey Pines Golf Course and the first time the U.S. Open would be held in Southern California since 1948. Torrey Pines was the first true municipal golf course to host this event in the 108-year history of the U.S. Open. This golf course is located on a beautiful cliff location, overlooking the ocean, and is the jewel of Southern California golfing. As a result of the selection, with two years until the actual tournament, the golf course management team and personnel were tasked with a complete renovation of the greens and fairways.

I could have easily assigned myself to the planning committee as the purchasing team representative. It was a high profile, important project for the City. At that time, USGA tournament organizers and officials estimated that hosting the U.S. Open at Torrey Pines would rank as one of the area's most lucrative sporting events ever, bringing millions of dollars into the local economy. They also felt that featuring the U.S. Open at Torrey Pines would demonstrate to the worldwide golfing community that public golf courses, where many golfers initially learn to play, can successfully host major events. The City's reputation was on the line.

But instead of assigning myself to the committee, I assigned this particular purchasing specialist. He was to serve as the purchasing representative, attend all meetings at the golf course, expedite expenditures, and oversee all purchases during the two-year effort to prepare for the U.S. Open. He absolutely loved it. I saw a new energy about him, and he started to pay better attention to his other work. Doing something he loved made him more productive and happy in his job. When the U.S. Open finally came to San

Diego, he attended all four days, coming within feet of some of the golfing world's legendary players. The joy on his face when he described the experience was hugely rewarding. And what a story to share with others about how he was part of the team that helped the U.S. Open be a hugely successful event for the City of San Diego. He became a part of history doing something he loved.

There are so many stories of how people working a "day job" achieved something spectacular. The Wright Brothers were simple bicycle makers when they thought of building a flying machine. Einstein wrote the theory of relativity while working in a Swiss patent office. Walt Whitman was a newspaper editor until he found fame with his book *Leaves of Grass*. By helping his teenage cousin with her algebra online, Indian actor Salman Khan later produced an amazing library of online lectures on math, science, and a host of other subjects. He ultimately partnered with Bill Gates on an insightful education program for classrooms across the United States.

So, work that day job...to pay the bills now. But the job should not hold you back. Continue to dream and work toward your Dream Life!

Chapter 6 Highlights: Working the Dream...Why is it so Hard?

Endurance class – contests where horse and rider traverse tens to hundreds of miles across rough country terrain and require great stamina and determination. Are you prepared to work for your Dream Life and do what it takes?

◊ Are you doing at least five things a day toward your goals?

◊ Are you working hard, or working toward your goals?

◊ What is the job you are doing now and is it your dream?

◊ Is your job part of your Dream Life or helping you get there?

Chapter 7

Changing Yourself to Grow Your Life

"We must look for ways to be an active force in our own lives. We must take charge of our own destinies, design a life of substance and truly begin to live our dreams."
Les Brown, motivational coach and speaker

Always be open to a learning experience. Travelling to new places, meeting new people, reading books or articles, watching documentaries, or trying new activities will change you in a meaningful way. If you are learning and changing, you are growing.

Being a Lifelong Learner

Benjamin Franklin once made an observation about many of the people he knew, "Many people die at twenty-five and aren't buried until they're seventy-five." Franklin was describing how people shut down their minds and quit learning. Have you met people who have not matured or grown past a certain point? Many people stop reading books after high school and college. Television or Internet newscasts are the only ways they stay informed about the world. They may go to the same places, hang out with the same people, and never really get out of their comfort zones. Many great comedy movies include a character who is frozen in time, usually around the high school years. This scenario makes for great entertainment, but it doesn't make a really good true life story.

A longtime friend has a great aunt who is a very loving woman. But she doesn't get out of her comfort zone. She hangs out with the same people, goes to the same lodge for dinner every Friday, and shops certain stores on regular days each week. When you visit with her, she has great stories and is fun to be around. But then on the very next visit, she is sharing the exact same stories. Nothing new has happened for her. It is difficult to discuss anything outside of her small town because she has no idea what the rest of the world is doing; nor does she have any concept of new or interesting topics. I enjoy visiting my friend's aunt, but I just know that we will be having the exact same conversation and I will hear the same stories that I heard ten years ago...it's almost as if she is frozen in a time warp.

So how do you become a lifelong learner? You have to be aware and stretch yourself. If it has been a long time since you have read a book, then read a book. Not a romance novel, but a book that will open a new world for you. Read a true story of perseverance or a book on a topic that has always interested you. There's the library, or downloadable free or low-cost books online..it's easier than ever to get access to books. Or there are a lot of great magazines on just about any topic you could dream of. If you want to travel, start reading about places you have often dreamed of visiting. If you want to start a new hobby, then start reading or learning more about that topic. If you want to know more about computers, or dancing, or learning a new skill, take a local class from the community college.

My husband is always interested in learning new things. Between the two of us, he is definitely the dreamer. Whether it's training German Shepherds, making beer, growing organic produce, studying early American history, or learning how to tie sailor knots, he is constantly ordering some book to read or researching on the Internet to learn more about a topic. I'm always amazed by how he is always so interested in exploring and learning about something new.

How many of us like to stretch ourselves in a new direction? Not very many...it can be uncomfortable. But go out of your way this week to meet a new person. Not a "Hi, how you doing?" "I'm fine" type of conversation, but really learn more about another person. While flying on business travel, I'm often tired and do not really want to talk to the person next to me. However, on those occasions when I have pushed myself to meet and learn more about the person next to me, I have met some very interesting people, including the owner of a large chain of restaurants, a litigation attorney who deals with disability issues, a young Mexican man who is the first in his family to attend college, an older couple celebrating their fiftieth wedding anniversary by going to Las Vegas for the first time, a nurse who is helping promote a new product that is saving lives, and a young man who is climbing the world's tallest peaks. Who have you met this week who is not in your regular circle of friends and family? Where have you reached out to talk to someone and learn more about him or her?

At our tasting room in Old Town, we have visitors from across the world who enter to enjoy a wine or beer tasting experience.

Upon starting a conversation, I always ask where they are visiting from. Often when they share their place of origin, I'll make a fun comment like "From Sweden...you are my furthest customers for the day!" Then people next to them may start to interject and say, "What part of Sweden...that's where my grandfather is from?" And next thing you know, both couples are talking and visiting. We literally had two occasions where two separate couples (one from England and one from Chicago) who did not know each other when they came in, found, after my introduction, that they lived within a block of one another back in their home cities...what a small world!

The famous business coach and speaker Jim Rohn once commented, "You are the sum of the five people whom you hang around with." I truly believe that. As a mother, there were certain kids whom I didn't want my children to hang out with. I felt those kids might be going down a wrong path or serving as a bad influence on my children. I didn't forbid my kids from seeing them, but I would often help steer them toward better choices, or encourage relationships with other friends whom I thought were more positive. We adults need to do that same thing in our lives. If you routinely hang out with people who just talk about the same things or never help to stretch you in new directions, maybe it's time to open up that social net a bit wider.

If you sat at the dinner table tonight with your family or partner, would you have something new or interesting to share? If you go two or three days without something new, then life starts to get stale...you start to get stale. Keep yourself fresh by being in a mode of learning and experiencing new things.

Eliminating the Clutter

Clutter is the stuff that keeps you from attaining your goals. And the clutter can take many forms—people in your life who drag you down, emails and television shows that suck up your time, or stuff that stacks up in your home and business to collect dust and prevent you from focusing on those activities or projects to help you achieve your Dream Life.

I'm an organized person, but on any given busy day or week, particularly when I'm travelling, stuff tends to stack up. Mail on the kitchen counter, magazines on the living room table, stuff around the house that doesn't find its way back to where it should be. I'm also the type of woman who has never had a maid. It's not that I can't afford one...it's just that I'm the type to clean the house before she shows up, so she won't know how messy we are! So, it's up to me to keep things organized.

Being organized has less to do with the way an environment looks than with how effectively it functions. If you can find what you need when you need it, and it helps you to achieve your goals, then consider yourself organized. In her book *Organizing from the Inside Out*, professional organizer Julie Morgenstern proposes a new definition that "organizing is the process by which we create environments that enable us to live, work and relax exactly as we want to. When we are organized, our homes, offices and schedules reflect and encourage who we are, what we want, and where we are going." Wouldn't that kind of organization support your goals?

Your way of organizing will be different than my way...but whatever works for each of us should be the way to go. Some people have messy desks, but if they can find what they need and are living full and enriching lives, then they have a system that works for them. So you have to ask yourself, "Is my environment supporting my goals and my efforts to reach those goals? Do I have clutter in my life that prevents me from achieving those goals or slows down my process?"

As I mentioned in a previous chapter, I cut down on television watching. It was clutter that was sucking away my time. I could sit in front of the television in the evening after dinner and literally 2-3 hours would go by before I would realize what time it was, and then I would decide just to go to bed. What a time waster. For someone who has a lot of goals, that was time I would have loved to use for more creative purposes. In another instance, I cut out some friendships with people who were not really contributing to my life or my goals. Though I use the word "friendship," I might need to redefine those relationships. If you have people in your life who are downers to be around, constantly filling your conversations with negativity, and not moving forward with their own lives, are they really good friends? Why are you spending your time with them? I am all for being a good friend and helping people when they are having rough patches in their lives...gosh knows, we all have them. But if every time you are around this person, it just drags you down, or you feel the person is never going to get past this bad spot, or grow further in his or her own life, then maybe it's time to detach a bit.

When I was a youngster, my dad was adamant that we all know how to swim. He would take my brothers and me to a local pond and teach the techniques he had learned as a former Navy pilot. One of our lessons was to learn how to save a drowning person. The idea is to grab the drowning person from behind, with your arm latched around his neck and shoulder, while you pull him and swim into shore. He cautioned that some people will panic when drowning and will not necessarily relax when you approach to save them. In their panic, they may start to grab and pull you down as if you were a life vest or log that will support them. It's not their fault...they are drowning and frightened. They really aren't trying to drown you, but they will if you don't take immediate action. We were taught that if that occurred, just to start swimming downward, and take the person with you. At some point, the person will panic that you are taking him down and release and let you go. Then you can rise to the surface again, just out of his reach.

If someone is dragging you down in your pursuit toward your Dream Life, my advice is to stay just out of reach to save yourself. Don't let another person drown you with a toxic relationship. I have a couple of colleagues whom I see at business gatherings, but I never spend much time with them outside those events. They are just too negative and always seem to be victims in all their stories, so I've eliminated that clutter.

During the last year, I also took a further step to eliminate the physical clutter in our lives by throwing or giving stuff away. It's interesting that when my husband and I moved into our four-bedroom home in the country with lots of large closets and a three-car garage, we thought we would never fill all the space. But with a busy life and three kids, all the corners quickly got filled with stuff. Even when the kids moved out, they didn't necessarily take all their stuff. They left it behind in Mom's house for safekeeping.

In her book *How to Manage Your Muck*, author Kathi Burns addresses the most obvious place to reduce clutter—the closet. She states, "where there is clutter, there is stagnant energy. Things cannot move, often literally." She goes on to explain that we often only wear 20 percent of the clothes we own. With an overfilled closet, it is easier to grab something that was just put back in. Clearing out cramped or cluttered spaces is very freeing, opening both the space in your environment and mind, creating more energy in the process.

Changing It Up

When was the last time you tried something new? Went somewhere new? Tried a new restaurant, or ordered a new dish at a restaurant where you routinely visit? Changed your style of hair or dress? We often resist change because it causes discomfort. We sometimes resist change because it can make other people uncomfortable. How many of us don't change our style or the way we do things because our partner, children, or boss would be uncomfortable. One time when my children were younger, I got a new hairstyle. When I went to school to pick them up, they just stared at me, and my son said, "You don't look like my mom." When my husband grew a beard, I really didn't like it. It changed my comfort zone with the look of the person I woke up with in the morning. But being open to small changes done consistently over time can lead to huge life-changing moments.

For instance, let's take something small. When you go to church or class, do you always sit in the same area or the same chair? Why? No one is making you...it's not an assigned seat. Why don't you change to a new location? Because it's uncomfortable! Next time you are in church or class, instead of going to your normal seat, go to a whole other section, and sit there instead. First of all, the view will be slightly different...same podium, same preacher or teacher, but just a bit different. Maybe you can see different choir members' faces, view the computer screen at a new angle, or appreciate the stained glass window in a new light. What's interesting is that the people sitting in their regular sections may look at you strangely and wonder why you aren't in your regular seat.

In our small church, my husband and I always sit on the left side about ten rows back. On one particular Sunday, we decided to switch it up...sitting on the far right in the third row. People actually approached us and said, "Why aren't you sitting in your regular seat?" and a couple teasingly questioned our motives. Motives? We were just sitting in a new seat at church. We were still participating as part of the service, but now we were making other people uncomfortable just by making a change. They wanted us to go back to our regular seats so everyone could be comfortable again.

Look around your house or apartment. Does it still look the same as the day you moved in? Except for maybe one or two new pieces of furniture you have added over the years, has it changed? Every few years, I feel the need to rearrange our bedroom. The bed and furniture have switched sides so often that I think we are returning to their original positions from ten years ago on this next rearrangement. My husband shakes his head, but he helps me with my ritual to change things around a bit. Have you ever changed your bedroom around? When you do, it's as if you are sleeping in a new room that first morning you wake up with the bed facing a new direction. I notice that particular corner of the ceiling, the way the light comes in through the window, my new view of the opposite wall. Getting out of bed demands taking a new path. There is no automatic pilot...you have to pay actual attention to the furniture's new location so you don't run into anything. Imagine how a small change like moving your bed wakes up your brain a bit and causes you to notice new things in a room where you spend almost half your time.

Do you always take the same path to work? I know I did. For twenty-four years, I had to drive to downtown San Diego, leaving our home, forty-five miles away, for that daily commute. After so many years, I knew exactly what lane to be in, which light would slow me down, and which right turn shaved two minutes off my commute. I could almost do that drive on automatic pilot. Sometimes I arrived home in the evening not remembering most of the drive home. I have lived in our small town of Ramona for almost fifteen years, but I travel the same roads to go to my regular places—grocery store, dry cleaners, feed store. I rarely go off the beaten path. However, when my kids were first learning to drive, we would take back roads to practice their driving skills. Whether it was dirt roads or back alleys, I learned more about my little town during those driving experiences than I had in all my previous years. We saw some beautiful horse ranches, a lake and reservoir, and campgrounds, and we found a great bakery. Some of the views were so spectacular that we would stop the car just to take in the beauty. There was always a new adventure when we went on those rides. Although my children are grown and no longer need driving lessons, I occasionally force myself to go down a road I've never travelled before, just for the adventure.

Travel is one of the best ways to open your mind, learn new things and have new experiences. Whether it is a drive to the next state or a cruise to an exotic destination, you will never be the same person after you return. My husband and I felt that travel would be a great educator for our children, expanding their minds and horizons to experience new foods and people, customs and dialects. When our kids were in elementary school, we took a two-week driving trip from New York City to Florida. Starting at Ellis Island, we visited Amish Country in Pennsylvania, toured underground caverns in Virginia, went to an Indian reservation in North Carolina, and swam in creeks in northern Georgia. Our children's minds were definitely opened. When my husband's father offered the kids "pie" for dinner...they didn't know that was New Jersey lingo for pizza. Travelling south, we knew we had passed the Mason-Dixon line when "sweet tea" became a regular feature on the restaurant menu. Our children still talk about that trip now that they are adults.

A couple of years ago, my husband and I took a trip to Yellowstone. It is a huge park, covering almost 3,500 square miles. We drove in the western gate from Montana and crossed the park to the eastern entrance in Wyoming, staying the night in Cody. The next day, we drove around to the north entry of the park and traveled southward to that gate, entering Jackson Hole and seeing the Grand Tetons. Each part of the park was very different, so I'm so glad we spent the time to drive through all four entrances. Mountains and streams in one part, steaming geysers in another, and the beautiful Yellowstone Falls and lake were all highlights. There was so much to see, and if I had missed one of the quadrants, I would have felt that I didn't get the full benefit of that wonderful American treasure.

If you aren't occasionally changing your environment, then you aren't changing. Take a trip to a place you've never been, drive down a new road, try a new food or rearrange your office—you will find your mind waking up a bit. If you always wear black, try some color in your wardrobe. Order something completely different off the menu at your regular restaurant hangout, or visit an ethnic restaurant to try foods never eaten before. Making small changes will open your mind. Looking at a project or your goals from a new perspective can be eye-opening. Fresh ideas and approaches will expand your horizon.

Chapter 7 Highlights: Changing Yourself to Grow Your Life

Breaking In – the early education of a horse, where it is taught the skills it will need for its future life as a riding, performing, or driving horse. Are you pushing yourself to learn new skills or explore new territories that open your mind and expand your knowledge?

◊ What are you doing to expose yourself to new opportunities or experiences?

◊ What physical clutter can you eliminate in your home or office?

◊ Are there people in your life who are dragging your down?

◊ What small step can you make to widen your experiences this week?

Chapter 8

Being Open to the Opportunities

"We are all surrounded by good luck and fortuitous opportunity. The difference between me and most everyone else is I STRIKE when it comes my way."
Richard Branson, world renowned business entrepreneur

Opportunities are all around us. What matters is whether we recognize opportunities or take action when they present themselves. Taking advantage of opportunities is the difference between those who achieve a Dream Life and those who wonder why they aren't getting where they would like to be. And opportunities don't often announce themselves, nor come delivered and wrapped up in a pretty bow.

Some opportunities come from misfortune...a lost job...a divorce...the death of a loved one. During those times, we may be so filled with grief or anger that we are blind to the opportunities. However, these moments sometimes push us to change or do something new we did not expect. When I look at my life journey, I often see specific moments that did not seem like a great deal at the time. I didn't see them as opportunities, but rather as new hardships. Those moments often took my life on a new path or trajectory toward something wonderful.

Opportunities sometimes come from persistence and hard work. It's amazing how lucky you get when you continue to get out there every day, pursuing your Dream Life and taking the steps to reach it. However, many people do not recognize this truism and give up when the going gets tough or the work becomes hard. Or as Thomas Edison once said, "Opportunity is missed by most people because it is dressed in overalls and looks like work."

One woman opened up an entire new product industry and billion dollar household name with no formal advertising, relying primarily on word-of-mouth. Sara Blakely, the inventor and founder of Spanx, grew up with humble beginnings in a small town in Florida. Her life's biggest pivot point was traumatic. While on a bike ride, Blakely witnessed her best friend being hit and killed by a car. In her grief, she turned to motivational tapes. Blakely said the motivational tapes changed the trajectory of her life, helping her to cope with challenge and disappointment, including when she later failed the LSAT entrance exam for law school. She admitted that failure started her on a different path. With no future in law, she ended up selling copier machines. It was hard work and often humiliating as people slammed doors in her face. But she learned a lot about sales and handling customers during this difficult period.

Blakely's next pivot point was much less traumatic. It started with a cream-colored pair of pants. She did not like how her panties created a seam underneath, so she spontaneously cut the feet out of her control-top pantyhose to achieve a smoother, more shapely look. Cutting the feet out worked to create a trim tummy and firm bottom, but the pantyhose rolled up at the bottom. Blakely wanted to figure out a way to keep them comfortably below the knee. She eventually believed she could redesign them to create a product that would be appreciated by other women.

Blakely decided to take $5,000 from her savings to develop "Spanx," a name she chose because the initial goal was to make a woman's butt look better. She started cold calling hosiery mills, but she was turned away. Finally, a man eventually returned her call. He had run the idea by his daughters over dinner, and they thought it was an excellent idea. They encouraged their father to call her back. The rest is history. Spanx began as a simple idea to conceal panty lines and cellulite, but it has evolved into a billion-dollar multi-product shapewear empire.

You have to wonder whether Sara Blakely would have developed this product and business if she had not had those earlier experiences or opportunities. What if she had not turned to motivational tapes after her friend's death? What if she had passed the law exam and become an attorney? The old adage, "When one door closes, a window opens" definitely applies in her case. Look at your own life and your pivot points or opportunities. Would your life be different—for better or worse—based on what path or opportunity you pursued after those pivot moments?

Looking back on your life, what have been some pivot points for you? What opportunities did they open or close for you?

_____

_____

_____

_____

_____

_____

Being Open to the Opportunity

Opportunities can come in big or small packages. Meeting someone at a mixer and learning that you both like the same breed of dog or have another similar interest might seem like an inconsequential occurrence. However, it is the start of a new relationship, and you never know where that might go. That person might introduce you to his or her friend who owns a large company that is looking for your services. A new acquaintance may invite you to a party where you meet the partner of your dreams. Trying a new activity may put you in contact with the social coordinator for a regional group who wants to buy your product or schedule a party or event at your location. I often have to remind myself that all great relationships start with a hello. A hello is how I met my husband. A hello helped to land my first job, and the one after that. It was the first thing I said when going to ranches to explore the Peruvian Paso horse world. Where "Hello" takes you is the unknown opportunity!

Here's a huge success story that started with a hello—"Hello Kitty" is a fictional character, designed by Yuko Shimizu and produced by the Japanese company Sanrio. Starting with a little vinyl coin purse—the first item ever produced bearing the Hello Kitty image—Sanrio later successfully attracted older females to the brand who didn't discover Hello Kitty until they were young adults. Products now include $25,000 Hello Kitty diamond-studded necklaces or $3,450 diamond and pink sapphire watches. As a brand and image that is recognized across the world, Hello Kitty is an example of a "Hello" that went global! You can sometimes find yourselves on the other end of a hello that can make a difference in your life or bring a new opportunity or relationship. I am often approached by people who come into the wine tasting room to ask questions about the wine or our shop. Or sometimes a salesperson introduces himself or a person comes in looking for a job. I always try to treat them respectfully and give them some of my time and attention. My last hired employee came in to apply for a job when I did not have one available. However, I took the time to talk with her, and we developed a relationship and rapport and kept in touch over a few months. When I finally did have a job opening, I had a ready candidate and did not have to advertise or interview to fill the position. If I had just brushed her off or not bothered to take a few minutes with her, I would have missed this great addition to our team.

I have a good friend who handles sales for a payroll company. She is a super sweet person and always open to networking and creating meaningful business relationships. Recently, a restaurant opened in her neighborhood and she attended the grand opening event and bought a small flower arrangement for the new owner to welcome her to the neighborhood. She left her card and asked whether she could call in the future for an appointment. The woman agreed. Two weeks later, my friend called the manager and set the appointment. When she arrived, the woman acted as if she did not want to be bothered and her behavior bordered on rudeness. My friend left the meeting with a very bad impression of the owner and the business. She stated, "It's okay that she did not want my service; I just wanted to introduce our company and learn more about her business." What this business owner did not know is that my friend is on the marketing committee for the local chamber of commerce and helps plan many of its events, which includes catering opportunities. She also lives nearby and would have liked to schedule their next family dinner at this restaurant. But as a result of the restaurant owner's rude behavior, my friend plans not to return, nor refer her location to others. What a mistake on the part of that business owner. You never know where your next opportunity may be coming from...sometimes, it is from someone who says hello to you. What you do from there is up to you.

Marketing the Ideas for Your Dream Life

Because we have a small family operation, my husband and I do not have a large staff nor an extensive marketing budget. Lack of resources, however, should never stop you from marketing or getting your brand or product known, particularly in this age of blogging, the Internet, and YouTube. In 2010, out of a group of several outstanding San Diego based companies, our family winery was awarded the San Diego Chamber of Commerce Small Business Marketing Award for the year.

How did we do it? By saying yes to every marketing opportunity we could create or find! Being in historic Old Town San Diego and dressing in historically accurate nineteenth century period costumes, we try to bring in a historical perspective. When we first opened our shop, we would bring our beautiful black horse in a horse trailer, and my husband would dress in a black cowboy outfit and ride around the park. He would hand out wine tasting coupons to those who came up to see the horse. And everyone wants to come up to a beautiful black horse—or handsome cowboy, as my husband would assume! I would be working in the tasting room, and guests would arrive with a coupon saying that a cowboy sent them over. We donated and poured wine at local charity events, featured local artists, hosted "Meet the Artist" evenings, attended business and women networking groups, and became active in the community. Our nomination package was hand-delivered with a wine bottle and red ribbon—just to make our entry stand out from the others. We were invited to the annual awards luncheon, along with all the other final nominees. When "Hacienda de las Rosas" was called as the winner, many people throughout the audience stood to applaud in support. My husband climbed the stairs to stand on stage in his full cowboy outfit, standing among all the other business leaders in conservative suits. He definitely stood out! Our goal was not to be the biggest winery out there, but to be the most well-known winery in San Diego County.

Creating your Dream Life requires marketing your ideas, goals, or business to achieve what you desire. If you want to be an author or publish a book, are you already marketing the book? Some of today's most successful authors start to market their books long before they are actually available. If your dream is to open your own business, what are you doing to start getting out there with the ideas? Are you talking to potential clients, searching for sites with realtors, connecting with services that might help your efforts, or researching the products to fill your storefront? Start marketing your idea before you even have a front shop door to open! If your goal is to be a professional singer, are you working with a voice coach, singing in small places, looking for a low-cost musician to play back-up, having publicity photos taken, and making professional recordings? No matter what your Dream Life entails, marketing your ideas and goals is part of achieving them. A whole world of people is out there, and many of those people can help to support your efforts.

There's an old children's church song, "This Little Light of Mine," that tells you not to hide your light under a bushel, but to "let it shine, let it shine, let it shine!" Your "shining light" will attract others to your ideas or cause, make others take notice, and open doors and opportunities. Shine your light...let it shine!

USA Today — We Made the Front Page!

One never knows who will be entering our wine tasting room. The visitor might be a tourist from Europe, a businessman from the Midwest, or a local person who hasn't been to Old Town in a while. We are always interested in who comes to taste our wines. One Saturday afternoon, we had a visitor who had been to our tasting room almost a year earlier. He was back in town for an annual convention he regularly attends. Earlier that morning, at his downtown hotel during breakfast, he met a reporter from *USA Today*. She was covering a couple of local stories in San Diego. He mentioned that he would be going to our wine tasting room later in the day, and he suggested that she should really try to meet him there to check out the place and taste some San Diego wines.

He arrived around noon and was telling us this story. Almost as if it were her introduction, Laura, the *USA Today* journalist, walked in the door. She was funny and delightful, tasting wines and sharing tales of some of the stories she had been covering. People were coming in and out of the tasting room, drinking and sharing... it almost felt like a party! When she started to leave, she asked whether she could include us in a business article she was creating, mostly around small businesses and entrepreneurs. Of course, we said, "Yes...as long as the article is a good one!"

A month later, a photographer came to the wine tasting room and took about 100 photos, and two days later, we were on the front page of *USA Today*'s Money section. It was amazing to see our picture on a publication that reaches 7 million viewers. We spent most of the afternoon driving around to find copies to buy. It was very exciting. The next day, we were checking into a hotel with our family to attend our son's graduation from boot camp. In the hotel lobby were stacks of the day old newspaper, so we quickly opened the page and showed our extended family members. Other hotel guests, including the front desk staff, gathered around as we all excitedly pointed to the article and our photo. The hotel manager even asked us to autograph a copy since he had never known anyone who was in a national paper before! So, the old adage of never knowing who you will meet is a good one...always be prepared and open to the opportunity!

Chapter 8 Highlights:
Be Open to the Opportunity

Opening – during a race, the rider will look for and take advantage of spacing between horses and the rail. Taking advantage of the right opening at the right moment can result in a win. Are you ready when an opening or opportunity presents itself and will you race toward it?

◊ What are some pivot points in your life that started you on a new path?

◊ What person or business would you like to meet or be introduced to?

◊ How many new people did you meet or what relationships did you try to nurture and grow this week?

◊ Are you marketing yourself, ideas, business, or your dream?

Chapter 9

Making a Plan B...then C...then D...

*"The majority of men meet with failure because of their lack of
persistence in creating new plans to take
the place of those which fail."*
Napoleon Hill American author

Not every dream is possible or plausible. I wanted to be a jockey
when I was little, but when I grew to over 5' 10", that dream was
obviously not in the cards. But behind the dream was my love of
horses. I wanted to breed and raise horses with outstanding blood-
lines—that was definitely doable. So my Plan B was to own a horse
ranch. My real underlying dream was to be around horses and to
own a horse-oriented business...it took Plan B to help me realize
the dream. Then we blended my dream of horses with my husband's dream of a winery and developed the family motto, "Drink
Fine Wine...Ride Fine Horses." That's an even better dream!

When Sally Ride was a young girl, she came home from school
a bit melancholy one day. As she recalls, there was not anything
specific bothering her—just typical teenager blues where she did
not feel as talented or as smart as her peers. Her father noticed her

mood and sat down to talk with her. He encouraged her to "reach for the stars." Knowing her achievements later in life, you might assume that hearing those words made her want to be a pilot or an astronaut. However, she decided her Plan A was to be a professional tennis player! Ride dropped out of school to take lessons and tour in the tennis circuit. Over some time, she eventually realized that she would never be good enough to reach the top ranks. So she went back to school and returned to her second love of science. Graduating from Stanford University with a master's and a Ph.D. in physics, she later beat thousands of potential candidates to enter the NASA program. On June 18, 1983, she became the first American woman in space as a crew member on Space Shuttle . She was later inducted into the National Women's Hall of Fame and the Astronaut Hall of Fame and was awarded the NASA Space Flight Medal twice. To be an astronaut was Sally Ride's Plan B!

When my husband and I wanted to open our winery at our home in Ramona, the local county ordinance required that an environmental impact report be completed at the cost of $250,000. After the money would be spent and the report completed, it still did not guarantee that we could open the tasting room. It was an onerous requirement since most small family wineries could not face this huge expense. As a result, very few wineries existed across San Diego County for many years. We decided to settle for a smaller operation, making some wine and selling it wholesale, which was allowed under the existing ordinance. In the meantime, we continued to work with others to change the ordinance, so that over time, we could eventually open our tasting room at our home and ranch in Ramona.

When you don't have a retail outlet or tasting room, it is a bit harder to get the word out about your winery and products. Since we can't sell directly to the public, many wholesale wineries participate in community events, donating and pouring wine to help with exposure and public recognition. On one particular occasion, we were invited, along with several other wineries, to participate in the Stage Coach Days celebration in Old Town, San Diego. This event commemorated the 100 year anniversary of the former stagecoach run from Tucson, Arizona to Old Town San Diego, California. The state park in Old Town was decorated with fencing, tents, old wooden tables, and cooking fires. All the participants were asked to dress in late 1800s attire. My husband and I set up our table and were ready to pour wine. On one side was a coffee grinder, and on the other side was a person husking and roasting corn. I had volunteered us to participate in the event because there would also be horses, carriages, and stagecoaches and saw it as an opportunity to see these horse-related activities. The evening was unusually hot, and I was wearing a stiff white blouse and long skirt with boots. The smoke from the nearby fires kept coming right into our booth, and my hair and clothes soon smelled like a campfire. Now I know why those women in the old black and white photos from the 1800s look so grim! The guests who came up to our table for wine never guessed how sweaty and tired we were. My husband and I kept smiling and pouring wine.

After the three-hour event, we were anxious to get home, so we started packing up our stuff to leave. The woman who helped organize the event came up and thanked us for attending, saying she appreciated our friendliness and positive attitude, despite the heat and smoke. Then she asked us whether we would be interested in exploring an opportunity in the Old Town area. By this time, it was late and my husband and I were covered in smoky sweat and just wanted to get home. So I politely took her card and said we would call her later. My husband and I almost completely forgot about this conversation until he found her card a couple of weeks later and said, "Do you remember what this lady was talking about?" I honestly couldn't and suggested that he call her. Once he did, she invited him to lunch in Old Town so they could talk.

On the day of his lunch, he called me excitedly on the phone and said, "You won't believe what she is offering...she wants us to open a wine tasting room in Old Town, San Diego." I just looked at the phone, thinking, "What do you mean, a wine tasting room in Old Town?" That was forty miles from our home and winery and wasn't even on our radar. He cajoled me to come down to Old Town, and when I did, he pointed to a plaza of shops and said, "She wants us to come here to open a tasting room, and we can choose whichever shop we want." She'd had this idea during the Stage Coach celebration, and since we had been so friendly and outgoing, she decided to offer this opportunity to us first. If we weren't interested, that was fine; then she would ask another winery. However, we were her first choice.

This was Plan B with a capital B! My husband and I talked about it for a few days. We would have to stop all our efforts on building our winery at our home and take that money and energy to open the new shop in Old Town. With the County nowhere near changing its restrictive ordinance, we decided to take a leap and open a tasting room within the city limits, where the only requirement was to file for a business tax license of $75. Let's see...pay $75 and open a tasting room within the city limits, or pay $250,000 for an environmental impact report, and still perhaps not be able to open in the county. So we pulled everything we had, maxing out credit cards and all our savings, paid for all the tenant improvements, and opened our wine tasting room in Old Town.

Opening a new business in the middle of a raging recession seemed like a big gamble. Opening a retail shop in a corner of Old Town that was not busy, but had great potential, was frightening. Taking on the responsibility and expense of a new business, while also trying to support three children who were entering college, was especially overwhelming. Once we opened the store, my husband and I worked there almost every day...he would usually open, with me working my government job during the day, and then coming over to close in the evening. We had one of our son's friends working as a part-time employee, and our young adult children helped occasionally on a shift or two. We worked seven days a week to get the business going. There's a saying about entrepreneurs—they will work eighty hours a week for themselves not to have to work forty hours a week for someone else. In our case, it was more like 100-120 hours a week between the store and the winery. It was almost non-stop. However, several years later, we now have one of the most successful and busiest tasting rooms in San Diego County. We have loyal customers, and folks come in who tell us they have to visit our shop every time they come to San Diego, which is amazing to us. People have served our wines at their weddings, anniversaries, family celebrations and holiday meals. It's special that our family product is part of so many special events. Five years after that opening, the County finally changed its ordinance, so we just opened a second tasting room at our winery and home in Ramona.

If we had stuck with Plan A, we never would have had a successful retail business for the past five years. We would have just continued our small wholesale business and waited for the County to make the changes over that long five-year period, so we could eventually open a tasting room. We would not have the large wine club and loyal customer base we have now. During the recession, we would not have made higher retail income, nor had the money to complete the winery building or pay for our kids' college tuitions. In hindsight, Plan B was better than Plan A, and it put us so much further ahead in our goals and toward our dream of freedom!

Was it easy...heck no! Plan B came out of a need to be flexible, take advantage of a unique opportunity, and ultimately, take a risk. Sometimes, I don't even know why I bother with Plan A because we never seem to get to do it. There is a saying, "If you want to make God laugh, tell Him your plans." I'm sure He has chuckled quite a few times at me over the years. My life lesson is that if Plan A ain't working, start rolling out Plan B! As long as you have your ultimate Dream Life in mind, who cares what path might help you get to it?

Life's Unexpected Surprises can Force a Plan B

In his book , minister and author Pete Wilson states, "The greatest of all illusions is the illusion of control." He shares that we all view our lives as if we are some type of marionette puppeteer who can control all the strings. A string to our kids, to our jobs, to our lives, and everything falls into place. And if we work and pray hard enough, we manipulate all circumstances to our benefit. However, a funny thing called life happens. Abruptly, your spouse may ask for a divorce, or your child may get in trouble, or someone dear to you suddenly dies. Business opportunities may come and go, jobs may be lost, or an unexpected illness might occur in your family. These experiences don't mean that your dreams go away. They may have to change a bit to reflect reality or the new environment in which you find yourself. That's when you form Plan B.

My husband and I had an unexpected Plan B a couple of years ago. During a routine physical exam, his doctor found that his PSA levels were slightly elevated, a warning sign of prostate cancer. Not really concerned, the doctor suggested that he wait another six months and then have his levels re-tested because test results could sometimes vary. For some reason, my husband, who hates to go to the doctor in the first place, insisted that a second test and biopsy be done. He admitted that he had a gnawing premonition that pushed him to make the request. The doctor referred him to a specialist who also was nonchalant about the results, but agreed to the biopsy at my husband's insistence. On the day of the biopsy, the doctor who was performing the surgery looked at the test results and said, "Why are we doing this procedure for a PSA level that is still relatively low?" My husband looked at him and said, "I'm already naked on the table, with a waiting anesthesiologist, so why don't you just humor me?"

A few days later, the results came back...six biopsies were taken and all six indicated prostate cancer. And not just any kind of cancer, but the aggressive T4 kind of cancer. Quickly, the doctor made arrangements for a full body and bone scan. When we went to his office to review the test results, he was very somber. He told us that the prostate cancer had metastasized to my husband's bones, spreading like barnacles on my husband's skeleton. He placed my husband's bone scan on the screen for our review and stated, "Everywhere you see black dots, that is where the cancer is located." When I looked at the x-ray of my husband's skeleton, it was literally covered in black dots. I turned to the doctor and said, "There are black dots everywhere." He nodded and said, "Yes, that's cancer on almost all of his bones." It was a shocking picture to view, and definitely not part of any of the plans for our Dream Life.

I have always been a "pull yourself up by the bootstraps" kind of person, so when my husband and I went out to the car, I became very matter of fact. We were going to live with cancer and not die with cancer. We were going to fight it, include it in our lives, and make our life be just as full—with or without cancer. Since that diagnosis, we have read dozens of books, changed our schedules and diet, met with specialists, and started on both traditional and non-traditional treatments. The doctor originally gave my husband an assessment of approximately two more years to live. Well, that was over three years ago, and my husband William is still alive and going strong toward our dreams. He has to slow down, take more naps, and sometimes has side effects from his treatments or days with pain. But it doesn't stop us from pursuing our dreams. William is still making new wines, and we just hosted the Grand Opening of a second tasting room with almost 450 people attending the party. With Plan B in full gear, life is good.

Switching to Plan B rather than giving up often leads to success. Growing up in South Korea, Do Won Chang worked in coffee shops. When he emigrated to California in 1981 at age eighteen, he figured hot joe would be his ticket to the American Dream. However, flashy Mercedes-Benzes and BMWs changed his mind and set Plan B in motion. "I noticed the people who drove the nicest cars were all in the garment business," Chang said. In 1984, he and his wife, Jin Sook, opened a clothing store named Fashion 21 in Los Angeles. His store took off, and as he expanded to other locations, the store's name was changed to its current title, Forever 21. The number of stores grew to 457 by 2010. In 2012, Forbes estimated Chang and his wife's net worth to be $4 billion. This company is one of the most successful female brands in the world. Chang lives in a $16.5-million home in Beverly Hills, never attended college, and describes himself as "as a simple Korean immigrant with a dream." Owning a coffee chain was his Plan A; however, it was Plan B, the clothing stores that helped him achieve his dream.

Plan B is not failure. It does not mean that Plan A was not a good or valuable plan. However, circumstance can change, and life brings different opportunities. The message is to be flexible enough to adapt to those changes. Altering and updating plans is both prudent and practical to move forward.

Chapter 9 Highlights: Creating a Plan B....then C....then D

Flying Change is the change of a horse's lead foot to rebalance during turns and changes in direction. Are you open to changing your plans when needed and developing an alternative path to reach your goals?

◊ When you look at your Plan A...is it working?

◊ Are you flexible to make a Plan B....or C, if necessary?

◊ What Plan B was forced upon you during your life?

◊ Does your Plan B help you continue toward your goals?

Chapter 10

Having Some Fun!

"If you obey all the rules you miss all the fun."
Katharine Hepburn, award-winning actress

Achieving one's dream is a lot of work. It takes sacrifice and time, resources and money, and a whole lot of energy to stay motivated. And it should also include some joy. Or else, why dream? Is fun a part of your life? I'm not saying that every day is a spa day or a ride on a roller-coaster, but do you experience moments of pleasure during your dream's quest? Are there times when you feel it's worthwhile or you have a feeling of satisfaction when you accomplish a baby step? If not, there needs to be fun in your dream. You define what fun is for you. I don't think skydiving would be fun, but for someone else, it's probably the ultimate thrill. Choose or create moments of fun during your life trip. Otherwise, it's all work and no joy.

Celebrating Your Baby Steps

Celebrate each milestone! Never wait to have a party! Each deposit in your savings account deserves a checkmark on the calendar and a hug from your partner. Each day without a cigarette deserves a smile and congratulations from your loved ones. Every step toward your goal should be documented and celebrated! When you get discouraged or have doubts, your record of past successes will quickly get you back on track. Celebrate each and every milepost on your path to your Dream Life!

It took almost ten years for us to open our wine tasting room in Ramona. Facing county ordinance restrictions, lacking money to build a functioning winery, and having to work full-time while building the business made the process go slowly. So, when it was finally time to open, we decided to throw a huge grand opening party! The event started with a Franciscan monk blessing our Spanish mission style building, which is modeled after California's first mission—San Diego Mission de Alcala. We invited a nationally renowned horse trainer to demonstrate his champion Peruvian Paso horses. International artist Robert Kidd offered to hang his exquisite artwork throughout the building. People stepped forward to volunteer during the event. Businesses stepped up with donations of raffle prizes. Over 400 people attended the weekend event, which set the stage for a very successful second wine tasting room.

Oprah Winfrey is known for her parties and celebrations. One party in particular was especially spectacular—The Legends Ball. This three-day event celebrated the contributions of African-American women who paved the way for younger generations. Honored guests were Maya Angelou, Tina Turner, Gladys Knight, and Cicely Tyson, and a younger generation of women, including Halle Berry, Janet Jackson, and Alicia Keys, joined in the celebration. The event was huge...starting with a Friday afternoon luncheon at Oprah's home in a gazebo built for the occasion, to a white

Accounting & Financial Women's Alliance

CONNECT · ADVANCE · LEAD

AFWA NETWORKING/SOCIAL

Brothels, Bites, and Booze: a Culinary Tour of SD's Questionable Past

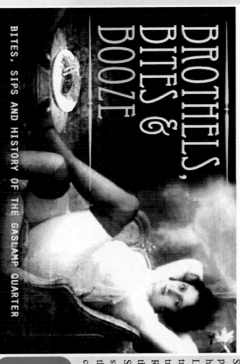

BROTHELS, BITES & BOOZE

BITES, SIPS AND HISTORY OF THE GASLAMP QUARTER

A walking history tour of San Diego's thriving New Town

Join us for a walking tour with SoDiego Tours that lets you explore the Gaslamp Quarter, the heart of America's finest city. Learn the secrets behind the district's historic buildings as you travel back in time to the post-Gold Rush era. Get an in-depth look at the infamous red light district. Satisfy your hunger as they make stops at popular restaurants. Finish the tour with a sample of a brew, cocktail or other intoxicating treat!

SAVE THE Date
Thursday, July 16th
6:00—8:30 PM

tie and gown ball on Saturday evening, finishing with a Sunday morning spiritual breakfast and gospel sing. Many attendees said the event made a huge impact on them. Oprah's goal was simple— to thank these trailblazers whose shoulders the successful younger generation now stands upon. During the Saturday evening ball, she commented that many people are celebrated and thanked after their deaths, but she wanted to pay tribute and say thanks while they were still alive. Her party gifts for the honorees were gorgeous diamond earrings. Oprah commented, "Was it extravagant? Yes it was. But considering what these women did to pave the path for me, it wasn't extravagant enough."

Your celebrations can be elaborate or very simple. Many people think you have to hit a huge home run before you can celebrate and cheer. But in baseball, every small step forward—a stolen base, a single or double, a great catch—is applauded. The overall goal is to win the game. However, the players and the spectators know that each hit, catch, and run makes that happen. The audience will clap and shout encouragingly throughout the game, and not just at the end. Lack of recognition is a common reason why people become disenfranchised in the workplace and eventually leave. It can also be a big reason why people stop working toward a Dream Life. If you are waiting until the end of the game (or life!) to celebrate, that's waiting way too long.

Sometimes, you can even turn a mistake or problem into an opportunity to create a fun moment. I travel quite a bit when speaking. No matter how much travel preparation is done, there are occasional problems with booking reservations. On one particular trip to Albuquerque, the rental car agency did not have my reservation. "No problem," I said. "Can I just book a car today?"

Apparently, there was a convention in town, so no economy cars were available. The manager was very apologetic, and said, "Would you like to rent one of our premium cars and I can give you a discounted rate due to our mistake." I looked over at the choices and there was a bright yellow Camaro convertible. I thought to myself, "Why not?" So I provided my credit card and went out to the car and immediately put the top down. When I pulled out of the parking lot, I realized my hotel was only two miles away—not even enough road time to take it for a real spin. So I thought, "What the heck?" and pulled onto the freeway. This was my first time in New Mexico and I had no idea where I was going, but I saw the sign to Santa Fe and decided to head north with the top down. I took the scenic route, toured the shops of Sante Fe, and enjoyed a picnic lunch at the park adjacent to the Cathedral Basilica of St. Francis of Assisi. I didn't head back to the hotel until after dark. And this all started with a rental car reservation problem! If I had gotten my economy car like I normally do, I would have probably just headed to the hotel to put in a few more hours of work for the day. But deciding occasionally to play "hooky" is a way to have some spontaneous fun too.

What have you celebrated in the past week? In the past month?

_____

_____

_____

_____

_____

_____

If you were to achieve one of your big goals this year, how could you reward yourself or celebrate with those special people in your life? Write it down and do it!

_____

_____

_____

_____

_____

Frivolity...in Wine Tasting?

Okay, so running a family business definitely has its ups and downs. One of the ups is that you get to see your family a lot...and that's a good thing. One of the downs is that you get to see your family a lot...and too much work and not enough play can be a bad thing. We try to schedule fun, without the work, but it's often hard to do. So occasionally, you'll come into the tasting room and find us joking and laughing, dancing to Aretha Franklin music, and having a good time while we work. If you want a quiet, studious, "foo-foo" tasting room, then we probably aren't the place for you. Wine should be fun...life should be fun...even when one works!

When guests enter, we offer a taste of our Sangria...sometimes red...sometimes white...and always a fun recipe. Guests are always surprised by how refreshing and fun it can be. But they don't get a taste unless they show some enthusiasm! When someone comes in, and we ask, "Would you like to try some Sangria?" and he just sort of shuffles or says, "I don't know," or "Okay," then I reply, "Nope, you can't have any" with a big smile. Then I follow up with "I spent time making this Sangria, and as a Mom, I want some appreciation for my hard work." The person then ends up laughing, smiling, and showing some enthusiasm to get that taste of Sangria. Funny, when it's free and easy, people don't appreciate it, but when they have to muster some energy, it's suddenly worth having!

Every Labor Day, our family winery hosts an old-fashioned grape stomp. We invite all our wine club members, along with family and friends, to our home and winery in Ramona. The event includes live music by a local band, grape stomping in a 120-year old California redwood tank, a huge team Jeopardy contest, and good wine and food. And each year, I keep the tradition of dressing as "Lucille Ball" from her famous grape stomping episode, one of my favorite of all her shows. With her mouth agape, Lucy stomped the grapes next to an Italian grape stomping woman who just didn't see the humor in the situation. It was a classic. Being a tall redhead, it isn't much of a stretch for me to pull off the physical appearance, with my dress that looks like a Bavarian pretzel girl's outfit. But the most fun is playing the part of Lucy...on that day, I can *be* Lucy... full of energy, making mistakes, laughing at myself, and having fun with others...it is completely liberating! I run around doing the chicken dance, jump in the tank, cajole people in the audience to join the competitions, and give the stompers some of the best moves I can create...there is the "sweep the floor...sweep the floor" motions, the military stomp, the Spanish flamenco moves, and my personal favorite—the disco duck. People have a great time watching, and of course, everyone has to have a picture with Lucy. If one put all the photos together that were taken of me that day, it could definitely serve as evidence that I was just a wee bit crazy! Everyone should be able to play Lucy (or any other wild television character) for one day a year...it is great therapy and fun!

Last night in the tasting room, we had mix of people—a small tour group from the Midwest, a large group of Meetup Hispanic business people, some wine club members, and guests who just happened in for a tasting. The room was loud, fun, and full of positive energy. It contained a whole cast of characters who didn't know each other coming in, but who had a great time mixing and mingling while they were there. Create the atmosphere of positive energy and fun...and you'll be surprised how contagious it can be!

Creating Fun in a Non-Fun Environment

You might be thinking...well, a wine tasting room, that's an easy place to have fun. What about where I work? It's an office setting and no alcohol in sight! Okay, but you can still create some fun. I worked for the City of San Diego for over twenty years, and believe me, government duties and the city council weren't there to make my life fun. So I created fun for myself and the teams who worked for me. When I oversaw the Community Service Center program, we would move our team meetings to other parts of the organization—beautiful Balboa Park, a newly built library, the wastewater treatment plant—and include a tour after the meeting. The energy was always high during those meetings, and lots of laughing and camaraderie developed among the teammates.

At the end of some of these team meetings, I would pose a question for each person to go around the table and answer. It would be a hypothetical question such as "If you could go back in history and meet anyone, who would it be?" or "If you had a whole weekend to yourself and money was no object, what would you do?" The answers were amazing and people were very thoughtful and sometimes funny with their responses. We got to see each other as real people, outside of the work process, which made us relate better as a team.

When I joined the Purchasing & Contracting Department as a purchasing agent, it was a place of low morale. Pushing paper through the bureaucracy, handling problems, and getting very little thanks were part of the job. However, I developed a set of visual rewards that put some fun back into this rather dull atmosphere. First of all...there was always a full bowl of chocolate in my office. Not cheap leftover Halloween candy, but really good chocolate. In the beginning, people were timid to come in, but as they grew more comfortable with me, they came in to grab a chocolate and touch base. Largely because of that chocolate, I informally learned a lot about what was going on in the organization, and I also got to know them as people.

On one large wall running the length of the office, I created a "Brag" wall. Every thank you note, complimentary email, or letter received I would post on the Brag Wall. And I would make a big deal out of them...reading them out loud or yelling out, "Wow... Sandra got a letter from the mayor's office...great job!" People would look out of their cubicles or come to the hallway, and of course, Sandra could hear me saying great things about her.... What a great way to add some fun. When I left that department after almost five years, that entire length of the 100-foot long wall was covered with messages. What a positive message for not only the folks who worked there, but visitors and vendors who entered our offices. It works for kindergarten teachers to have a bulletin board...why not for adults at work?

During our monthly team meetings, I would hand out the "guppy" awards. These were colorful stuffed fish I would hand out to recognize people for efforts that went above and beyond during the past month. The person could choose his or her favorite fish, which were then proudly displayed in offices across the floor. When visitors asked about the stuffed fish hanging on people's walls or sitting on their desks, employees would share how they had received the guppy award.

After a time, I decided there should be another award...one that each peer could give to another. However, it had to be a special one-of-a-kind award where only one person at a time would receive the award. I had a huge stuffed fish at home—really, I don't know why my awards were all fish-related!—so I took him to work. At the next team meeting, I announced that I had a huge new award, but it was very special. The first time it would be awarded by me, but the next time, the recipient of this giant fish would then decide who the next awardee should be. The fish would be given to someone who helped you personally or really made a difference in your life that week. I then gave a short speech about the young IT guru who had completely redone my system and made my life heavenly after my computer was working. I handed it to him and said, "Here are the rules for the fish. You must award this fish to someone else in the department within the next three days. It can't wait longer than three days because we all know that fish start to stink after that length of time. And after you deliver it to the person, you will send out an email to the entire purchasing team (almost 100 people) to let them know who is receiving the fish, and what that individual did to make a difference in your work life that week." Well, he took the fish to his office and proudly hung him on the door. And three days later, he sent out an email to the entire department sharing a good news story about the fish's next recipient, who had helped him on a project that week. This process of sharing the fish went on for almost two years. Every three days, a person would receive the giant fish and an email would go out.

At one point, I really wanted someone in the warehouse to get the fish since the warehouse staff wasn't in the office with the rest of us, but they were definitely part of the team. But I couldn't direct someone to give them the fish because that would undermine the fish's message that each recipient determined where the fish would go next. So I could only hope that someone would give it back to me. And finally that day arrived—the fish was mine! So I called Walter, a big burly worker in the warehouse district, and asked him to stop by my office on his next delivery downtown. When Walter came to my office, I asked him to sit down, and then I explained the giant fish award. Walter looked at me kind of funny. I excitedly told Walter that he was the new recipient of the fish. Walter stared at me, and in his thick New Jersey accent, he said, "I don't want the fish." I looked at Walter incredulously because EVERYONE wanted the fish! He stood up as if the conversation were over. I also stood up and said, "Walter, you don't understand...this is a good thing!" and continued explaining what the giant fish award was all about. Walter started to back toward my office door, still looking at me a bit strangely, and said, "Nah, that's okay; I don't want the fish." Then I stated in my sternest loudest tone, "Walter, you are going to take this fish, and in three days, you will give this fish to someone else, and write an email to the whole team explaining why they received the fish...do you understand?" Walter nodded, stepped forward and sheepishly took the fish.

He then turned to go, but as soon as he left my office, I heard a voice down the hall yell out, "Hey, Walter, you got the fish...

congratulations!" A couple of other people then yelled out "Good job, Walter!" At that moment, Walter's stature changed...he stood a bit taller, tucked the fish under his arm, and strutted a bit, replying, "Yeah, I got the fish!" Three days later, I arrived at work, thinking I was going to have to remind Walter about passing on the fish and sending out an email. Imagine my surprise when I opened my email box to find a three-page long email from Walter to the entire team. It entailed his three-day adventure with the fish...it went to a Padres' game, on a date with his wife, and each night, the fish was placed next to his fish tank before he went to bed. And he ended his email saying, "It's not fair that the fish doesn't have a name. I decided to name it after my best childhood friend Tony." And from that day forward, he became "Tony the Fish."

On the day I left that department, I was packing my boxes and had put Tony on top of the last box. People were coming by to wish me well, but they were dismayed to see that Tony was going with me. In fact, I started to feel like they were going to miss Tony more than they were going to miss me! At one point, I thought about leaving him behind. But then I thought with a new director coming in, he would want to develop his own tradition. It was also up to the team to continue creating its own fun in the future. In fact, I heard that once the new director learned about Tony, he started his own "Hot Chili Pepper" award. In every circumstance, everyone has to create his or her own fun!

As entrepreneurs, with very busy schedules, my husband and I must schedule fun for ourselves. Whether it's a movie and dinner out, or a short trip away, we have weekly and monthly goals to get out and have fun or take some down time. And fun doesn't have to be a huge event. When we recently went out of town on business...we snuck away for an evening of quiet...ordering a movie and room service in the hotel room and not answering any phones or emails. At one point, we actually looked at each other at the same time and said, "This is fun!" almost as if we were playing hooky for a few hours.

Because we make a concentrated effort to commit to fun, we are also aware when it isn't happening. In fact, with no fun or breaks for a while, one or both of us starts to get a bit cranky. Some weeks, we are more successful than others; occasionally, a couple of weeks will go by where we didn't schedule some fun or time away from work and responsibilities. We then work to rectify the situation by scheduling some down time or fun. In the end, it makes us better partners, business people, friends, and parents.

Over the next week, what fun are you going to schedule for yourself? How about the next month? Year? Achieving a dream or living a life without any fun is a dull existence.

Name a fun activity for yourself this week:

_____

_____

_____

_____

What is something fun you can do with your partner or friends this month?

_____

_____

_____

_____

How can you start adding some fun to your workplace? What is something you can start today, or introduce that would help make your work area a more positive place to work?

_____

_____

_____

_____

_____

What is a big fun activity you would love to do this year? How could you start planning for it?

_____

_____

_____

_____

_____

The Fish Philosophy

On a visit to Seattle, John Christensen observed how animated and happy the employees at Seattle's Pike Place Fish Market were in their work. They filled orders by flinging fish to each other, inciting laughter from the customers and compliments about their throwing/catching abilities, or commiseration if they missed. Employees would often invite customers to join the fun. The Pike Place employees gave their complete attention to each of their customers and ensured each had an enjoyable visit. Christensen realized that not only were the workers making a routine errand fun for themselves and their customers, but they also were selling tons of fish.

He constructed the FISH! Philosophy from his observations of Pike Place employees, which includes a very successful book and video. His concepts include having fun and choosing your attitude each day.

Every activity and every duty that you must complete is not necessarily fun. Some days, we have to do the stuff that stinks. Or we have to complete tasks that are menial or boring. But regular doses of fun can help make those moments the minor parts of our lives.

Chapter 10 Highlights:
Having Some Fun

Play Day is an informal, social competition featuring games and activities where horses and riders can learn and compete in fun. Are you including fun in your life, and is it part of your Dream Life?

◊ Have you had any fun this week?

◊ What have you recently celebrated?

◊ Can you incorporate fun as part of your schedule?

◊ What activity or idea can you add to your workplace to create a more fun atmosphere?

Chapter 11

Putting People Before Stuff

*"Let us endeavor so to live that when we come to die,
even the undertaker will be sorry."*
Mark Twain, author

I am a big believer that people should always be more important than stuff. Many of us have witnessed firsthand how families and friends are torn apart by fights over money, stuff, and all things tangible. In the end, it really never is the "stuff" that matters—it's the people, and our relationships, memories, and experiences with those people. It is interesting that many people learn this lesson, often late in life. However, it would be great if people could learn this lesson so much earlier in their lives…they would be so much richer and happier for it.

I had a distinct visual of this reality upon the deaths of two grandmothers—two very different women. The first grandmother was a very distant woman, not known for any warmth toward her children or grandchildren. She came from a very wealthy family but married a farmer. While they weren't wealthy, her things and money were still very important to her. All the furniture in her house was double covered with furniture covers, so they would never be stained. Plastic runways were placed from room to room so people would not walk on the carpet. She had dishes that were displayed and would never be used, and parts of the house were always off limits. When her grandchildren visited, they were more comfortable staying outside to play. Going inside would be followed by constant instructions on where to sit and what not to touch. When this grandmother had a stroke late in her life and was admitted to a home and then hospice, almost no one went to visit her. She had little to no communication with anyone. At her funeral, only a few family members attended and less than a dozen people from the small community where she had lived almost sixty years of her life.

At the other end of this spectrum was my Granny Munn. Granny Munn grew up as an orphan, cared for by her grandmother, and lived in poor farming conditions most of her life. She had four children and nineteen grandchildren whom she cherished, regularly showing them her love and affection. When anyone came over to visit, whether family or neighbor, Granny would cook up a meal of whatever she had…catfish caught that morning, greens from the garden, or a dove that she had just de-feathered. My cousins, brothers, and I could come and go in Granny Munn's house, helping ourselves to cookies and spending the night whenever we were in town. Her door was always open. When Granny Munn passed away, the little brick church in that small Florida town was packed. Sitting on the pews were not only her daughter and three sons, but most of her grandchildren, who flew in from all over the country, friends from church, and even people from the nursing home where she had spent her last few years, after suffering several debilitating strokes. And the most surprising attendees were the ex-wives for each of my ever-marrying, ever-divorcing uncles. Not for the benefit of their ex-husbands, but for the love and respect of this woman who had loved their children and always welcomed them into her home. Granny was poor by any national standards; when she passed away, she had no real assets to claim. However, her legacy lives on through her children and grandchildren, and she is still remembered fondly to this day.

My mother Lessie follows the same philosophy. Visitors to her home are always welcome, and people often share how much they love being around my mother. Her recent birthday party was attended by over 200 people. That is a true testimonial to someone who puts people first. When a guest comments that he or she feels comfortable or welcome in my home, it is a high compliment. I have learned from the lessons demonstrated by my grandmother and mother before me.

With the plethora of reality shows, I rarely ever watch television anymore. I would rather live my own life than watch others live their lives on my television screen. However, when staying in a hotel, I sometimes scan the channels to see whether there is an old movie or anything worth watching. On one particular evening, I was fascinated by one show, *Cheapskates*. This particular show highlights people who put saving money above everything—family, friends, and even their own well-being. It is fascinating to watch the extremes they will go to in order to save money. Now, I tend to be cost conscious myself, and I understand the importance of saving money. But what I find so sad in these shows is that these people have so few meaningful relationships. And in those few relationships, the other people feel so devalued and taken for granted. It seems unfortunate. While the "cheapskates" are saving all that money, they are losing so much more. And what happens when they save all that money? What happens if they finally reach the goal of saving the magical amount? They aren't going to spend it anyway. If you gave a cheapskate a pile of money, he would just save it and never spend or enjoy it. Even the Bible says that the "love of money is the root of all evil." Saving money is an admirable trait, but to let that completely define and rule your life means that you are loving money more than people.

Think of all the people in your life who have helped you along the way...did you thank them? Do they know that you appreciate them and what they have done for you? For someone who helped or befriended you when you were growing up, did you go back later and tell the person how much he or she meant to your life path? It's amazing that many people don't know how they have impacted others, but they are sincerely touched when someone thanks them for the difference they made in that person's life. Are you a grateful person who shows appreciation to those who either help you today or have helped you in the past?

My oldest son is extremely bright. At age two, he knew the entire alphabet and had cognitive skills beyond his years. However, he had difficulty learning to read. While he knew his letters, he could not put the letters together in any meaningful way to learn to read. Even though he was tested, there was no sign of dyslexia or other physical impairment. As he entered the school system, he started to fall behind. It was not because he wasn't smart. He was actually one of the brightest children in his classes. He just could not focus to make the letters make sense. I remember sitting across from his former first grade teacher during a parent-teacher conference as she went through a litany of what he was not capable of achieving. I interrupted her at one point to ask, "Do you even have one good thing to say about this child? Can you even any of the talents and skills that he does have?" I was so incensed that I demanded the school district place him in another classroom. My child was not going to be around this woman who put him down on a daily basis.

He was then placed in a class with an incredible teacher, Mrs. Bartel. She had a classroom full of children with different capabilities, and she worked with each child at his or her own level. Always positive and supportive, she saw each child's capabilities rather than deficiencies. She recognized that my son was very creative and visual and that he absolutely loved comic books. She asked me to send him to school every day with one of his comic books. She took his passion—comic books filled with action packed stories and pictures—and used that as an avenue to teach him to read. Over time, he began to read the comic books on his own, and then he moved to the classroom books. Now as an adult, he is a voracious reader, reading everything from *War and Peace* to the Bible. When my son graduated from high school, I tracked down Mrs. Bartel, who had already retired, and sent her a bouquet of flowers with his high school graduation photo to thank her for helping him to find his own way. I will always be grateful for what she did for my son.

Was there an adult when you were a teenager who served as an example or gave you advice that you can still hear today? How did that affect you at the time? How does it help you now? If you could thank that person...would you? Most people like to be thanked and appreciated. You would be surprised how many teachers, coaches, or team leaders love to hear from former students in a positive way. Do you have a former supervisor or mentor who made a positive difference in your career path? Does he or she know, and did you say, "Thank you"? Maybe it is not possible to go back and thank the person now. But have you thanked anyone this week? Is there someone with whom you work or live who supports you, helps you, or has done something recently for your benefit? If so, say, "Thank you!" It's free and it's easy. It is one action that truly shows people in your life that they matter.

When I was a supervisor, I routinely wrote thank you notes. Not an email nor a text message, but an old-fashioned handwritten thank you note. No one writes thank you notes anymore. They take time and energy. And because no one does them...they are special. I wrote a thank you note for someone who helped me prepare a city council presentation that went well. I wrote a thank you note to an executive secretary who went the extra mile to help coordinate a meeting with attendees from various locations. Thank you notes also went to my peers and superiors within the organization. I wrote a note to the fire chief after the Witch Creek fires for her hard work and dedication on behalf of the residents of San Diego. I wrote one to the mayor when he took a stand for something that I also personally believed in. And you know what? People appreciate those notes. I've gone into people's offices and seen my notes sitting on their desks or on their windowsills. I've gotten thank you notes for my thank you notes because they meant so much to the recipient. Heartfelt thanks expressed in a personal note can mean a lot and take very little time. During your life plan, make sure to thank and appreciate the people who help or encourage you along the way.

We all know takers in our lives—the people who never come around nor talk to us unless they want something. Whether it's a family member, coworker, or salesperson...they are there to get what they want and not offer much in return. You start to dread when they come around and go out of your way to avoid them. Then there are the givers. Those people who are generous with their time, their energy, and their resources. They are often the first to volunteer or offer to help. And these people are often referred to as the "good" people in life. Unfortunately, because they are givers, they are sometimes taken advantage of by the takers. Sometimes they lose money to the takers, or they are given more work and less credit, or are not in the spotlight as much. However, at the end of my life and on any given day, I want to be known more as a giver than a taker.

Giving before taking is one of the greatest things a person can do...in a relationship or business. Our winery's business plan includes giving as an integral part. For instance, we often donate a gift basket, bottle of wine, or gift certificate to charities for their fundraisers. At least once a month, we will volunteer to pour our wines at one of their fundraising events...a case of donated wine can go a long way to help. In addition to the gift, we often enjoy mingling with others who are givers and donate their time and efforts to the organization. When we opened our tasting room in Old Town, I wanted to host the artwork of local San Diego artists. On any given month, we feature their artwork, host a "Meet the Artist" reception, and have their business cards and information available for interested patrons. Sometimes we receive a call from people who want to take photos at our winery and horse ranch for their holidays cards, or want to come by to let their disabled child pet a horse. Why not give? It is so easy and it makes us feel good.

Have there been takers in our business? Yep, they are everywhere. I had one lady call, requesting a donation of ten cases of wine for her charity event. This was a cold call on her part...she had never been to our tasting room, and she didn't want to come to our winery or visit in person. I explained that we were a small family winery, and would love to contribute, but ten cases was more than we could afford to one charity. Each case had a retail value of $250, so that would be a $2,500 donation. Since this particular charity has nationwide recognition with a list of benefits for larger donors, I asked whether we could qualify for some of the benefits and recognition as a large donor. She got huffy with me, and said, "Well, your wine doesn't cost you anything, so why can't you just give it away?" I tried to be patient and explain that the grapes, bottles, corks, labels, and capsules all cost money. My husband's time, sometimes over the course of several years, was certainly worth something. At that point, I declined her gracious offer to take ten cases of "free" wine from us. Sometimes, I admit I do draw the line with some takers. But on the whole, we always try to give *way* more than we ever take.

In looking at your own life, are you a regular giver? Not just of your money, but your time? The giving can be related to your business or to an area of interest. If you are good with animals, maybe you could volunteer at the humane society or a feral cat program. Or if music is your thing, how about volunteering to play, perform, or teach lessons at a senior center or a high school program that needs assistance? There are always community activities listed in the paper or on Craigslist looking for help or volunteers. We all have full lives, and it is difficult to find the extra time or energy, but you will be surprised how good you feel after making the effort. Studies have shown that givers tend to be happier people. In one experiment, one group of people were given money to spend on others, while a second group was given money to spend on themselves. In the end, those who had spent money on others were much happier and more satisfied. Doling out money isn't the secret to happiness, but being open to giving of your time, resources, and money can open you up as a person. As a side benefit, it may also present opportunities or experiences that you never would have been exposed to otherwise.

I once had a boss who really liked to hobnob with the top people of every company whom we worked with. However, I noticed that if the "fish" weren't big enough...he wouldn't spend any time with that person or show any interest. He wasn't rude, but you could tell that he couldn't be bothered with the smaller fish in the pond. There was one particular company that he was seeking to partner with in business. He had been trying to meet with the company's vice president, whom he had heard would be the decision maker. When we were at a trade show, I mentioned that particular company had a booth at the trade show too, and he might want to go introduce himself. He walked up and saw a young woman working the booth. Apparently, he thought she wasn't high enough on the food chain, so he walked by and didn't stop to introduce himself. At the end of the conference, he found out that the young woman *was* the company's vice president. She was the very person he had been trying to meet with for almost a year. And even if she hadn't been the VP, it still would have made sense for him to introduce himself to learn more about the company and possibly gain insight and show respect to the person who was there. I've watched him enter a room and always head to the highest ranking person. I personally believe he is missing out on a lot by this approach. People in the middle and even at the bottom are just as important to any organization. When I was the department director, I used to tell people that I could leave for a week and things would run fine. However, if the receptionist or payroll specialist left for a week, the whole operation would come to a grinding halt! Each person has a contribution to make, and no one should be slighted or overlooked because of job classification or responsibilities.

Have you heard the story of the janitor who helped create Frito-Lay's hottest selling product and become one of its top managers? Richard Montañez worked as a janitor at the Frito-Lay Rancho Cucamonga plant in California. Call it luck or a craving, but Montañez said it all began when he saw a corn man at the fair adding butter, cheese, and chile to the corn. He wondered, "What if I add chile to a Cheeto?" It was an idea that would make him a legend. Richard experimented in his mom's kitchen, grabbed some spices, and made a test. His friends and coworkers loved it, so he called up the president of the company and said he had an idea for a new product. He was granted a meeting, with two weeks to prepare his presentation. With no background in marketing, he copied a marketing strategy from a library book. "I'm a little bit of an artist so I even designed the bags and put the Cheetos in it," Montañez explained. The president loved the idea and since then, the Flamin' Hot product line was born, including Flamin' Hot Cheetos—which is Frito-Lay's top selling snack. Today, Montañez leads Multicultural Sales & Community Promotions across PepsiCo's North American divisions.

How about the story of the grandmother who walked across the country and then ran for political office? At age eighty-eight, Doris "Granny D" Haddock, a widow who had never held political office, decided to take on the system by walking across the whole of the continental United States. She went door-to-door to advocate for campaign finance reform that would help ensure that people could become involved in politics, even if they didn't have millions of dollars to spend on their campaigns. After two years traveling the nation, she finished her journey in Washington D.C., where she was escorted to the Capitol by dozens of members of Congress to the cheers of thousands. Several years later, Granny D decided to run for a New Hampshire U.S. Senate Seat, challenging the Republican incumbent. Although Granny D didn't win the race, in the end, she attracted widespread support, capturing 33 percent of the vote and the admiration of millions. Her political campaign was documented in a fascinating HBO film, *Run Granny Run.*

Never underestimate the power of someone with a dream. When you acknowledge someone, you recognize that person's value and importance. Go out of your way to acknowledge people. Make an effort to "see them." Like the Na'vi in the movie *Avatar*, who greeted one another with the phrase "I see you," it is a message of respect. Actively listening with deep interest signifies that you really care about what someone is saying, in contrast to simply listening because it is the nice thing to do. If you question whether people can tell the difference, they can, and it matters. Just as you wish to be acknowledged, appreciated, and heard, do so with others. Let it start with you.

Chapter 11 Highlights:
Putting People Before Stuff

Tack is the gear used on horses such as a saddle or bridle. Who takes the priority and attention in your life—stuff or people?

◊ What do you value in your life?

◊ Who are the people in your life whom you cherish?

◊ Have you thanked someone today? Can you thank someone from your past?

◊ Is there a way that you can share your resources or time to help others?

Chapter 12

You Can't Do It Alone

*"I'm thankful to my family, friends,
and fans for all of their support."*
Serena Williams, Tennis Champion

We have all heard the expression "It takes a village to raise a child." That same expression can be applied to building a Dream Life. It actually takes a village or support system of friends, partners, family, customers, and businesses to help achieve any Dream Life. Who are the people in your life with whom you spend the most time? Have you shared your dream or passion with them? Did they laugh at you, or were they supportive? Is your partner or family supportive of your dream? Will they help or be cheerleaders to encourage you on the path to your goals?

My husband and I have a good family friend, Vince Biondo, who has a successful contracting business, a loving family, and a wide circle of supportive and close friends...some all the way from high school. When Vince was young, he often played the drums with different bands. However, as his kids got older, and his business took most of his time and interest, he moved away from something he was passionate about. Just before he turned sixty, Vince was invited to play with a band. His wife, Laurie, was completely supportive, as well as his best friends, so he jumped right in. Lo and behold, he loved it, and he quickly remembered all the old rock and roll songs he had played so many years before. He now enjoys going to gigs on the weekends with the band, and he even played at his sixtieth birthday party for all his guests. No one's face had a bigger smile than Vince's that day as he banged away on the drums!

Think of the people in your life—in both your professional and personal life—whom you spend the most time with and put them in the categories below:

Supportive:

_____

_____

_____

_____

_____

_____

Not Supportive:

_____

_____

_____

_____

_____

Now, make a list of the types of people you want to attract into your life. If you want to be a writer, do you want to hang out and be friends with other writers or publishers? If you want to be a chef and own your own restaurant, do you share interests with people in this same industry who might help you? If going back to college and getting a degree is your goal, who will help support you during this period when you need a babysitter for your children while you attend class? Write the names or types of people you would like to attract into your life:

_____

_____

_____

_____

_____

_____

Thomas was an eight-year-old sickly child who struggled with partial deafness. Academically, he lagged behind his peers, and his teachers continuously ridiculed him for his perceived slowness. One day, Thomas returned home from school with a note from his school principal. The note stated that he was being expelled from school due to his slowness and poor academic performance. His mother, who saw his potential and was his biggest supporter, responded by teaching Thomas at home within a loving and accepting environment. Soon, Thomas started to develop a new appreciation for learning, and he began devising new inventions. Decades later when Thomas died, America honored him by switching off the electric lights throughout the nation for one minute. Yes, I'm talking about Thomas Alva Edison, inventor of the lightbulb and phonograph. Imagine where we would have been if Thomas had not experienced the love and support of his mother.

It's okay to ask for help. Being an independent person and a very hard worker, asking for help is something I personally struggle with. I often assume that if I just work hard enough and long enough, my goals will be reached. In hindsight, I wish I had asked for more help, or paid experts in certain areas where I was not particularly skilled, to move my goals and dreams forward in an expedited fashion. For many years, I did all the bookkeeping, taxes, and bill paying for our family business. And I hated it. It was tedious, boring, and took time away from doing what I really liked to do. Two years ago, I met a bookkeeper, Shirley Guiducci from ERA Accounting, through a women's networking meeting. She showed me some accounting shortcuts, such as keeping my expenses online and creating P&L statements on a quarterly basis. Over time, I started to give many of these duties to her, paying for her expertise and time. Due to Shirley's help, by February of each year, we are ready to file our taxes. This is a huge accomplishment compared to my past struggles to get everything done by April 15th each year, and hating life during that final week before taxes. I should have asked for help in this area years ago!

When my kids were small and I was working full-time, I wanted to obtain my Master's degree in Public Administration. It was the only way I ultimately could be considered for a director position. These were the days before online classes were available, so I personally had to attend class, as attendance was often part of the grade. So, I asked others to help me—from picking up my children from school to babysitting while I attended class. It took me almost six years to complete a two year master's program, but I did it. I could not have done it at all without the help and assistance of others.

If people ask you, "How can I help?" do not immediately turn them down. Think about it, and see how they might help with your goals. They have offered themselves. Why not take them up on the offer? Maybe they could introduce you to someone who can help you achieve one of your mini-goals, or they could offer their expertise in an area that isn't in your skill set. Or they could listen to your ideas and help make suggestions. We are sometimes too quick to say, "No, that's okay" when someone offers his help. Next time, say, "Yes," and see what door it may open for you.

Another type of "ask" is for business. We often do such a good job creating our product or service, marketing it, and trying to sell it, but then sometimes we forget to ask for the order. When a customer completes a wine tasting in our store and comes up to the register to pay, we often ask, "Which was your favorite wine, and would you like to take home a bottle?" Or we might mention our wine club and how the customer's tasting experience could be free if he joined today. And very often, the person says, "Yes!" I don't know whether the person would have decided to purchase the bottle or join the wine club without the suggestion, but why leave it up to chance?

As a purchasing director, I have sat across the table from vendors and heard hundreds of sales pitches. And some people never ask for the sale. They will give a perfect PowerPoint presentation, show the reasons why their company or product is so great, and then thank me for the meeting and leave. Even with government rules and bidding processes, people can still talk about how to purchase through other government contracts or share how other customers are using their services. Now that I'm outside that role, I often coach company salespeople on how to ask for that government sale. It's the final and most important part of the process. Otherwise, the sales call is just a storytelling exercise, and then hoping for the best.

Great teams and athletes who achieve the highest awards often credit their coaches with helping them to reach their goals. Coaches help you strive for higher heights. That's why many people hire a personal trainer to help with their fitness goals. A coach will push you harder, hold you accountable, and develop new strategies to push you through tough points. We hired a branding expert, Liz Goodgold from Red Fire Branding, to help with our winery tasting room business. While we were satisfied with our progress to date, we wished to take it to the next level. With a fresh set of eyes, she reviewed our current business processes and marketing strategies. Building on our great customer service and family brand, she had us reevaluate some of our current tactics and try some new ideas. Small changes led to our revenue almost doubling over the course of the year. And we learned to delegate more duties to others, instead of doing it all ourselves. This gave us a bit more down time, which actually led to more creative thinking of new business ideas and strategies.

Asking for help is not a weakness. It's an acknowledgment that there are others who have skill sets you can use or learn from. Receiving these gifts from others can take you, your business, or your life to higher levels. So, get your "ask" in gear.

Chapter 12 Highlights:
You Can't Do It Alone

Herd is a social grouping of horses when in the wild or together in a pasture. Are you part of a herd who supports you and your dreams?

◊ Who are the people in your life who are supportive or not supportive?

◊ What types of people do you want to bring into your life?

◊ Is there someone who has offered help or you can ask for help?

◊ Do you regularly ask for business, new ideas, or introductions as part of your marketing strategies?

Chapter 13

Being the Leader of Your Life

*"A Good Leader inspires people to have confidence
in the leader, a great leader inspires people
to have confidence in themselves."*
Eleanor Roosevelt

Tons of books and articles have been written on the art and science of leadership. Each author has his or her theories and strategies for being leaders of businesses—big and small. However, the type of leadership discussed in this chapter is how *you* can be the leader in creating your Dream Life. You have to be the leader of you...who else will do it? Most of us aren't going to have our goals just handed to us...we have to lead ourselves...our lives...the people around us toward that goal.

Being True to Yourself

I once worked for a boss who talked a lot about ethics. But over time, I witnessed him being less than truthful in some of his interactions. He would often tell one version of a story to one person, and then another version of the same story to another person just to get what he wanted. Observing this behavior, I really lost respect for him, making it difficult for me to follow his vision. When I was growing up, my mother was very adamant about keeping one's promise. If she promised something, then whatever it took, she would keep that promise. I followed en suite with my own children, so they knew when they heard the words "I promise," they could count on it. I might sound like a kindergarten teacher, but ultimately, your promise is your word and must be kept.

In pursuit of your Dream Life, you have to be true and ethical to yourself. You also have to appreciate and value the skills and talents you bring to the table. You can change a bit to match the situation or circumstances, but you ultimately have to be true to your nature, to your culture, and to what resonates within your soul. I'm a very friendly, outgoing person, but that often doesn't play well in a stuffy corporate or government setting. In the past, when giving presentations, I would strive to tone it down a bit, or wear the boring black or brown required business suit. But over time, I realized it wasn't me. So, on city council presentation days, I decided to wear my brightest red suit, or add a story as part of my presentation. And you know what? I actually became a better presenter. While being professional and respectful, I was also being myself and developing my own style. There were some "old school" government types who didn't appreciate my style, but I got lots of compliments from others. Most of the time, my agenda items were approved by the city council. I believe the council members could sense that I was being authentic and truthful...they believed what I was presenting. And because of my storytelling and sense of humor in my presentations, I started getting invitations to speak. If I had stayed in the mold I believed was expected of me, I never would have received the speaking opportunities that have come from across the country. Whether it is speaking at a national conference on government procurement or sharing stories about the wine industry of San Diego at a local networking group, I enjoy sharing my knowledge in a fun and informative fashion.

Be Glad to Have a Glass!

We've all heard the expression that pessimists view the glass as half-empty, but optimists view it as half-full. However, I've met people who are so negative that they complain about the glass itself! Nothing is ever just right, and most of their conversations are a long string of one complaint after another. I have a former friend with whom I had to cut off any interaction because of her negative attitude and complaining about the "glass." Every single lunch together was almost painful as she complained about her job, her husband, her debt, her car, her house, the economy...you name it! No matter how many times I tried to change the conversation to something more positive, she would follow up with a complaint or another downer story. Over time, I spent less and less time with her. I eventually stopped seeing her because of how exhausted and drained I felt after any interaction with her.

Are there people around you who attract other people because of their vitality and positive energy? What do you like about them? Do you look forward to seeing them, or plan activities that include them? Can you be yourself with them, and do they appreciate and like you as you are? How about at the other end of the spectrum— those people who can just suck the energy out of the room just by being present. Do you know any of those people? How often do you hang out with them? Is it by choice or obligation?

Life is too short to hang out with constantly negative people—I want to be the person who is happy to have a glass...no matter whether it's half full or empty, I've got a glass! And it's amazing how positive energy is contagious. Conversations are filled with affirmations and "feel good" stories, with a lot of laughing and supportive sharing. And you feel energized after interactions with these types of people.

I'm not a "Pollyanna." I've had my share of bad moments or sad occasions during my life. However, I encourage you to strive to have your life's balance sheet filled with more positive moments and activities.

A positive physical element also exists in laughter and happiness. A good belly laugh opens the diaphragm, increases circulation, releases endorphins, and helps build a stronger immune system. Science has proven that laughing is good for your health because it lowers the stress hormones cortisol and adrenaline and increases endorphins and human growth hormone. A great side benefit is that it also burns extra calories and tones the facial and abdominal muscles. Children often laugh hundreds of times per day, while adults' daily laughing spells reside in the double digits.

When travelling, it amazes me how irate and stressed people can be at airports. The noise and lines, the delays and slowness of loading and unloading passengers, intrusive security checks, and large crowds in small places...it's enough to make anyone tense. However, I literally tell myself to "take my brain out" during these times. The goal is not to stop thinking, but to stop reading too much into a situation and just relax. So when the TSA agent is taking forever to go through the screening process, I figuratively take my brain out and wait patiently. If a woman comes on the plane with three suitcases and holds up the loading process, I take my brain out.

Two weeks ago, I sat next to an engineer who was clearly becoming agitated by watching people put their suitcases in the overhead compartment and taking up way too much room. He didn't think they were being efficient. I could hear him muttering about how their bags should be stored. I quietly leaned over and told him that I took my brain out during these times. He quickly smiled and said, "Yes, I need to take my brain out right now." During those moments when I feel the stress start to rise, I call my husband or kids to tell them I love them before taking off, or I pull out a book or magazine to preview, or I start to count some of my blessings... anything to take away the pressure of that moment. Does it always work? Of course not...I'm not a saint. But I can say that more often than not, I've learned not to sweat a lot of the small stuff!

Forgiveness to Help You Move Forward in Life

When I worked for the City of San Diego, I was acquainted with a city planner who was part of an incredible story of forgiveness. My former colleague, Ples Felix, was raising his teenage grandson Tony. Despite all his grandfather's efforts, Tony became involved in a gang. In 1995, during a botched robbery attempt, Tony killed Tariq Khamisa, another young man who was delivering pizzas that afternoon. Every parent's worst nightmare is that his or her child will be killed or hurt through violence. When Tariq was killed, his father Azim Khamisa went through extreme depression and questioned why his aspiring son, who had just taken the pizza delivery job for a little extra spending money, had been killed in such a senseless act. However, ten months after Tariq's death, Khamisa told the *San Diego Union-Tribune* that he had made a conscious decision to forgive the alleged killer. Within a year after the murder, Khamisa started the Tariq Khamisa Foundation, which teaches the virtues of nonviolence to young people across the nation.

In the meantime, Felix was supporting his grandson through the legal process and trial, and also praying for a way to help Tariq's family. He was not only supporting his grandson through his trials, but he struggled with finding a way to reach out to the Khamisa family, whom his grandson had harmed. At some point, Ples approached Azim to convey his sorrow and remorse over the death of Tariq. Azim greeted him with reverence and the two talked for a long time. After that, the two men became very close friends. They joined together to support the Tariq Khamisa Foundation and give presentations across the nation about their story. In time, Azim went to the prison to meet Tony, the young man who had killed his son. They began corresponding, with Azim offering words of encouragement and support as Tony served his term in the prison.

This story always amazes me. I think of my own children and know that if anyone ever harmed them, it would be very difficult for me to forgive that person. For some reason, I have a better skill set at forgiving those who hurt me, as opposed to those who hurt my family, but I am working on it. Nelson Mandela said, "Resentment is like drinking poison and then hoping that it will kill your enemies." Here is a man who served over twenty-seven years in a South African prison, subjected to discrimination, beatings, torture, and abuses of all kinds. But he rose to power and worldwide acclaim due to his ability to forgive and move forward.

Each one of us has experienced words or trespasses against us that have traumatized or hurt us. Everything from school day taunts to real cases of abuse, from others' trivial missteps to outright lies and deceit from those whom we trust or love. If you live any type of life at all, you are going to be hurt in the process. It does not make it any easier knowing that, but at least you know it is part of the process of living. So, what do you do with that hurt? Do you push it down and ignore it? Do you retaliate and get back at those who hurt you? Is it something that prevents you from moving forward in certain areas of your life...with business...with relationships... with your family?

I know people who hold onto hurts like they are badges of honor. I have a former acquaintance who constantly complains— about his job, his coworkers, his partners, his bosses—the list goes on and on. And he is quick to anger; he seems to remember every infraction that was ever done to him, and he always has to have the last word in any argument. Unfortunately, as a result of holding on to that hurt and anger, he doesn't have much of a life. He doesn't have a long-term partner, has a minimal social life, hates his job, and suffers from depression. He is extremely bright and can be quite funny, but his unforgiving nature holds him back from enjoying all the possibilities that life can offer.

Forgiveness is never about the other person...it's all about you. If someone has hurt you badly or physically abused you, I'm not saying that you have to forgive and stay in an abusive situation. What I am saying is that you do have to move in a positive direction...maybe even moving away from that situation, relationship, or even severing ties. But in doing so, the forgiveness part is for you. It's for you to move on with your life...not necessarily to trust, love, like, or even interact with that person again...but to forgive and take control of your future. The person who hurt you should not have the opportunity to control your life. Forgiveness is an action. It is a step in a positive direction for you and your life.

Being a Good Manager of Your Life

Good leaders have vision. They know where they are going and what they want to accomplish. To be a good leader of your life requires some good management as part of the process. Management of your time, your focus, your resources and money, and ultimately, the ability to hold yourself accountable. How are you managing yourself now? Do you plan your time, what gets spent on the "must do's" of the day, and the time that goes toward your Dream Life? Have you created systems to keep track of your goals, your baby steps toward those goals, and the resources that must go to support your effort? Have you done something today or this week to move you toward your Dream Life?

Discipline is what is required. This word gets a bad rap. It is generally used in a negative connotation such as "Discipline that bad child" or "You can't lose weight because you have no discipline." However, it should be looked at as the means to accomplishing your goals. Who decides what you are going to do for the day? You do! Okay, your boss expects you to be at work at 8 a.m., and your kids need you to pick them up after school, but you are the one who ultimately decides to complete those tasks. You also decide whether you stop for coffee and spend $4 on a cup, or you make a quick cup at home. You decide what path you drive to and from work, the time that you leave, and what you wear for the day if you don't have a required uniform. All these little decisions are made by you. And some are good, meaning they help you move toward your

Dream Life. And some are not so good when they take you away from your Dream Life.

For instance, what if your dream is to be able to travel on a worldwide cruise within the next two years, completely paid for in cash. That goal requires money to pay for the trip, a passport and possible visas, coordination of who will take care of your pets or children during your absence, and the ability to leave your work or business for that length of time. Are you taking all the baby steps to reach that ultimate goal? Saving the money to make the down payment? Setting aside or working toward a certain amount of leave time to have enough time on the books before you have to request the thirty days off? Getting ready for this big trip takes planning and discipline.

Now imagine if your trip is your Dream Life. The way you want to live, where you want to be in your career or business, whom you want to be with are all parts of that dream. Are you taking the steps, week in and out, to work toward those baby steps to achieve the goals? Are you making yourself get out there to meet the right people, save the money, do the work that's required, and market what you are selling. Discipline is how people achieve anything big. When someone loses over 100 pounds, she has made those daily decisions on when and what to eat for the length of time it takes to lose that weight. If someone wants to have $10,000 in savings by the end of the year, he starts putting aside money each week or month. That is discipline—setting the goals and then doing what it takes to achieve them.

Having a dream is almost easy. It's the day in and out management of your life toward that dream that is the hard part. Everyone must develop a system with some type of accountability to measure his or her progress within that system. Your system is different than mine. I love lists and goals that are written down...as I check them off, then progress is made. Others might like hiring a coach or partner who helps develop the goals and keeps them on track. If you don't have a system, you need to develop one. And if you do have a system, you routinely need to review and determine whether it is helping you get to where you want to go.

What system(s) do you have in place right now to help you achieve your goals?

_____

_____

_____

_____

_____

_____

_____

Why does this system work for you?

_____

_____

_____

_____

Why is this system not working, or what do you need to have it do for you?

_____

_____

_____

_____

What can you change, starting today, to make the system help you move toward your Dream Life?

_____

_____

_____

_____

_____

In the end, it's up to you to manage your days, weeks, and months. Look at it this way: If you only had one year to achieve your goal, would you be acting differently? Are you pushing yourself a bit, making yourself try new things, becoming a bit uncomfortable? You have to lead and manage yourself at the same time. A leader will present a vision, and the manager will develop the steps to reach that vision. In this case, you have to be both.

Chapter 13 Highlights:
Being the Leader of Your Life

Alpha Mare is the lead female of a herd who determines the best route to travel, when to move from one place to another, and claims the right to drink first from watering holes. Are you leading your life or letting others lead it?

◊ Is your current life and style true to your own personality and values?

◊ In your life today, what or who are you grateful for?

◊ Is there someone whom you can forgive for a past transgression?

◊ Do you have a system in place to hold yourself accountable and measure your progress toward your goals?

Final Thoughts

Why Not You?

"Your time is limited, so don't waste it living someone else's life."
Steve Jobs

Strive to be extraordinary, not just ordinary. I'm not talking about being rich or famous, or even recognized by many. I'm talking about being noteworthy in your own life—to your family and friends, and to the people in your circle of influence. Are you making a positive difference? Are you living a fulfilling and happy life? Are you pushing to do new things at every stage of your life? What is your Dream Life? Why not go for it? Why not now and why not you?

The struggle to stand, then fall, then stand again has a long history in the animal kingdom with newborn animals. When a young horse is born, it usually lands with a plop, covered with the film of the amniotic sac and the umbilical cord still attached to the mother's uterus. The mare will often nudge the baby to rise, and encourage the foal to start moving. In the wild, the mother is aware of the dangers of a newborn becoming the next meal for a nearby predator. Getting the baby to move is necessary for its survival. As a human watching this event, there is often the temptation to run in and help the baby to stand and start nursing. However, letting the baby learn to stand on its own, and more importantly, learn how to get up again after falling, is essential. The baby's little brain is learning and trying new things that will imprint for the future.

The same occurrence happens when children are trying something new. Whether it is learning to ride a skateboard or ride a bike, there is a lot of trial and error in the process. While parents can lend their advice and a helping hand, in the end, it's the child who must learn how to balance him- or herself and have the gumption to get up again after a nasty fall. Adults sometimes get out of practice of this natural routine of trying something new. We try something once, and upon failure, decide it is not something we can do. However, often it's the process of trying, failing, and trying again that can make us successful.

How many times or how long should you fail at something before you quit? Well, if you asked Henry Ford, he might reply, "At least a year or more." He asked his engineers to create a one-piece eight-cylinder engine, to which they replied, "It can't be done." He argued that it could and set them to work. After one year of failures and an insistence that it was not mechanically possible, he insisted they keep trying. Finally, they succeeded. When in 1961 President Kennedy stated that a man would be on the moon by the end of that decade, many did not even know how it might be done, or even if it were possible. However, NASA worked the next few years, with some of the best scientific and engineering minds on the project, and made it become true.

It's hard to achieve a dream. If it weren't, then everyone would be living his or her dream. It's frustrating, scary, exhausting, and a lot of hard work. And it's also exhilarating, rewarding, and takes the best that you can give. The best achievements are like that—whether it's being a successful parent, businessperson, artist, or inventor. That's why those people who achieve their dreams are successful, or happy or recognized...because only a small percentage of people live what they dream.

Many people seem to wait for their lives to start. There's a country western song sung by Tim McGraw entitled "Live Like You Were Dying." It is sung from the perspective of a person finding that he has a serious health issue and might not have much longer to live. So he starts to live life—becoming a better husband, a truer friend, and taking on activities such as bull riding and skydiving. His message is succinct when he says not to miss a moment and to treat tomorrow as a gift.

Life is happening. If you are just going through the motions and living the daily grind, that's just being ordinary. You are special and unique. You should not wait around hoping that others will identify your special talent or uniqueness. You need to identify it for yourself and treat your life as something special. What are you going to do for the rest of today? What is going to make this week special? When you complete this year, what are you going to look back on to appreciate or be proud of?

Be yourself...your extraordinary self...starting today. Drink Fine Wine and Ride Fine Horses is my Dream Life—what is yours?

About the Author

Tammy Rimes is living her dream life of running a winery and horse ranch in San Diego County. Having worked as an employee in the corporate world and later as a Purchasing Agent and civil servant manager in city government, this chestnut-haired entrepreneur knows what it is like to feel locked in. More importantly, however, she discovered how to take off the blinders to face head-on the fears and obstacles preventing her from living the life of her dreams. She took her passion for horses, with her husband's passion for wine, and created a lifestyle for her family. As a consultant, author, and speaker, she is now on a mission to show others how they can create their own Dream Life.

Made in the USA
San Bernardino, CA
03 June 2015